In My O

A pocket atlas for life's journey

Michael Kelly

For Ron & Carol

x

Michael

© Michael Kelly 2006

All rights reserved. No part of this publication may be reproduced in any material form (including photocopying or storing it in any medium by electronic means and whether or not transiently or incidentally to some other use of this publication) without the written permission of the copyright owner except in accordance with the provisions of the Copyright, Designs and Patents Act 1988 or under the terms of a licence issued by the Copyright Licensing Agency Ltd, 90 Tottenham Court Road, London, England W1T 4LP. Applications for the copyright owner's written permission to reproduce any part of this publication should be addressed to the publisher.

Warning: The doing of an unauthorised act in relation to a copyright work may result in both a civil claim for damages and criminal prosecution.

A CIP Catalogue record for this book is available from the British Library.

ISBN 10: 1-905633-01-7
ISBN 13: 978-1-905633-01-2

ISBN 1-905633-01-7

9 781905 633012

Published by Etica Press Ltd, Malvern, Worcestershire, England
Printed and bound in Great Britain by Peartree Press

Foreword

By Rolf Harris CBE

My wife Alwen and I have been great friends with Michael and Dee Kelly for something like twenty years. They actually live just down the road from us. Michael asked me to have at look at the manuscript of *In My Opinion,* to see what I thought of it, and possibly to suggest any changes. I was delighted to do so, although the changes suggested were minor and few and far between, but I thought the content was marvellous, and my enthusiasm prompted Michael's suggestion that I might like to write this short foreword.

He tells me the book was not written for profit and was simply an opportunity to say what he's always wanted to say about what he's learned about life. By so doing he hopes that future generations, (his own in particular), might have a better start in life after consulting his "pocket atlas for life's journey". I believe it achieves his objective.

Passing on one's experience to the next generation in book form must be good. Perhaps we might all consider doing the same one day, for everyone has learnt some of life's lessons, and preserving this learned wisdom can surely only improve future lives. This probably looks and sounds a lot easier than it is. Any attempt to immortalise one's inner thoughts takes some courage, because your own personal convictions are then on display for evermore for all to see and to criticise.

I found almost all the subjects he expresses his opinion about to be of great interest to me, and I would imagine his opinions would be of practical interest to all ages. Many of his observations have certainly provoked thought from me, and sometimes amazement. I find his casual style is refreshingly candid and gently humorous, interesting, as well as being philosophical, and there were whole areas that I knew absolutely *nothing* about, which were a revelation to me. He warns of pomposity at the beginning because anyone having the nerve to write so openly and personally about his own views on politics, religion and sex might otherwise be thought of as pompous. But obviously, the book will only achieve its purpose if it *is* frank and honest.

Michael has always been an enthusiast for everything he tackles, and if there is one theme that shines out, it is his aptitude for positive thinking. He commends this positive approach to all, for solving many of today's problems, problems to do with health, happiness, business and even mental illness. I do have a worry that not all his readers have the same capacity that Michael does for always looking on the bright side of life, and maybe a few of his proposed "solutions" may be unreachable for some, but what a joy to have all these alternatives put before you.

I have to confess that the financial and business parts worried me until I started reading them. *Then*, they started to make sense in an area that had always terrified me. I just wish that I had read these sections of the book when I was starting out in life. I may have found these subjects less frightening to me today. I'm sure that a youngster thinking of starting out in business will profit from these fascinating and hugely revealing areas.

It is a book worth picking at and there are a number of interesting sections outlined in the *Contents,* which can be selected at whim. Having said that, the opening section on the *meaning of life* does set the scene for what follows and could well start the first argument!

Finally, Michael's wife, Dee, features in the book from time to time and he makes no bones about the fact that she is clearly the power behind the throne. He refers to her as the "upper house" and she is obviously a great influence on Michael, and, from what we know of her, rightly so. Their marriage is wonderfully blessed and an inspiration to us all. I hope their grandchildren will eventually get around to reading this book. I am sure that they will find it a very valuable and well-thumbed pocket atlas.

Rolf Harris

Bray 2006
www.rolfharris.com

Introduction

Before you bother to search for the author's biography on the back flap, let me save you the trouble and tell you straight away who I am and what this is all about. By the way, the list of contents is on page xi. But first things first.

My name is Michael Kelly, age 60 something, and I currently live in the lovely Thames-side village of Bray in Berkshire with my beloved wife Dee. I am somewhat opinionated and certainly a trifle pompous, a family trait apparently. I have three children: two came with my marriage to Dee over 37 years ago, and one we baked ourselves. We have a handful of grandchildren, with hopefully more to come. This little book was mostly written for them. But, for anyone else who might want to scrutinise their own attitudes to life, they also might find it helpful to examine and criticise another person's perspective, possibly agree with some of the views and probably argue with others.

I have had a very fortunate, happy life, a great marriage, a successful business career and have struggled over the inevitable hurdles that arise from any eventful voyage. I have certainly learnt a few lessons along the way. Life is always surprising. Had I listened and observed more when I was younger, I might have achieved more, but who listens to crumbly old grandads? Hindsight is easy, but I wish I had paid more attention to my elders.

I thought I would make this attempt to write down some of the key discoveries I have made so far about people, their interaction with each other and with this complex and sometimes puzzling planet on which we all make an uneasy attempt at co-existence. And what a comparatively short existence that is, taken in the context of the life of the universe; we exist for just an eye-blink compared with the vast time span of the cosmos, from its "Big Bang" some 14 billion years ago when it all began to...well, whenever it all ends. We have to make the most of this tiny sliver of time we call our own life, because we are dead for far, far longer.

My scribbling might just assist my grandchildren start out a little better equipped than I was – if, unlike me, they pay any attention, or possibly their parents encourage them to, and always assuming my opinions turn out to be legitimate in the end. I am still learning too. The more you learn, the more you realise how little you know. The sheer size and extent of this amazing universe can be daunting. But by possessing a crude map drawn up by a previous traveller, hopefully suggesting a few interesting detours, must surely be more useful than just aimlessly trampling around life's huge park, bumbling into dead-ends and sometimes missing out some of the best bits. Much is obvious but still need saying.

I have little time for extremists. Dee thinks I am an extremist. She thinks I can be obsessed with things and get carried away on a whim while excluding and ignoring everything and everyone for a while. She might be right occasionally, but I think I am simply an enthusiast. I do get excited about things. I admit that this enthusiasm can occasionally *seem* like an obsession and yes, I am occasionally carried away a bit as you will read, but despite all this, I sincerely hope this missive was worth the effort.

Dee also says I lecture rather than converse. Didactic I am told (I had to look that word up). OK, possibly guilty. But I still prefer to think that it is my innocent excitement whenever I discover something, some new principle, or "a fact of life", perhaps an unlikely truism. I then need to share my excitement with anyone who will listen. To me, life really is fantastic fun and my curiosity about it seldom tires. In fact, my inquisitiveness increases with age, although Dee thinks I sometimes act as if I am only 14 years old. In reality, it is merely childish excitement, born out this impulsive urge to explore and analyse until I get to a satisfactory conclusion.

My childhood was a happy one, although I was fatherless for my first 10 years. My mother then married Jim Kelly but I failed to click with my new stepfather. I was interested in technical things and he was interested in fishing and football. We had little mutual respect then, although looking back I realise I was a selfish little brat and should have been more respectful to his genuine attempts at being a father. He was actually very kind. It was only when I became a stepfather myself that I realised how difficult it is to bring up someone made from different clay from you.

With no meaningful father image on which to base my fledgling persona, I had to invent one, adopting attributes that attracted me from the myriad characters that impressed an immature youngster in the 50s. I definitely wanted to be an action man. I loved Superman (black and white in those days) and American action movies. I also liked exploring. I thought I might like to be a philosopher, although I probably could not even spell the word at the time.

I loved thinking and inventing. Still do. I also enjoyed making cranes, engines and cars with my beloved Meccano set. I was more at home with logarithm tables than football league tables. I have always had an open mind and love to challenge any and all philosophies. Dee says that I am stubborn and just like arguing. "Typical Taurus" she says. Maybe I over-used my perceived role as the family leader, demonstrating that I was firmly in command by taking important family decisions and then sticking with them. ("Even if they are wrong, darling?" says Dee. Well, we mere men have not quite achieved that level of wisdom that women annoyingly seem to have built in at birth.)

Actually, although it may seem as if Dee's opinion is sometimes at odds with mine, it is not really so. She is probably the wiser of the two of us. She should really write this book. However, I do check things out with her. It is a bit like getting a bill passed through the House of Lords, she being the Upper House that can reject the Bill, but the House of Commons (me) could still push it through if it wanted, or dared to. So this book is actually a sort of joint effort, although I insist on getting the credit of course. I have already scrubbed one section completely on "advice" from the Upper House.

In the 50s, it was thought to be terribly bad form to discuss politics, religion or sex, particularly when ladies were pres-ent. Moreover, my parents felt that meal times should be silent; a legacy from Jim Kelly's family who did the same thing for generations back, believing children should be seen and not heard. This was sad, as I was very keen to talk about those very subjects and to test my own unsophisticated opinions on the waiting world. But that was how things were in those days.

Robert Louis Stevenson said "It is better to travel hopefully than to arrive". I relate to that. I think that it is more the *climbing* of a mountain where the excitement lies, rather than reaching the pinnacle and simply planting a flag. Arriving at the summit and gazing back down at the twisting, tough track on which you have travelled certainly evokes a grand feeling of achievement, even if there were many difficulties en route, more *because* it wasn't such an easy journey. I prefer to revel in a stimulating and adventurous voyage. One might even die *before* arriving.

Having already climbed a long way up this mountain, I thought it worthwhile to record some of good and bad routes I have experienced. Life is abundant with potholes into which we all fall from time to time. My aim is to reduce the chances of any fellow explorers taking a similar tumble – provided that is they take the trouble to consult this atlas, which incidentally points out some of the scenic routes too.

There are no chapters in this treatise, just a few random sections you can pick at. Sometimes a specific thought-thread can be bundled into a unique segment on its own but may be too brief or too trite to pose pretentiously as a full chapter. So to save the embarrassment of having to blow up a mere paragraph into a drawn out episode, I have abandoned chapters altogether.

Anyway, what follows will be the ramblings of a 14-year-old granddad, naively thinking someone might want to listen to his philosophy of life. Well, it is only *my opinion*. I can but point – it is up to you to look.

Beware pomposity

For the avoidance of doubt, every sentence in this book could have been prefaced with the words "In my humble (read pompous) opinion ..." but it would be terribly tedious to do so. Although it may appear as if I am pontificating, let me state now that everything said herein is just **my opinion**, right or wrong, unless occasionally accredited to someone else. While I still reserve the right to be tedious, at least please judge the validity of my arguments with an open mind: I may very well be hopelessly wrong on occasion. (I did think I was wrong once, but it turned out I was mistaken.)

Beware simplicity

A good joke starts with a story and ends up with the punch line. A text book should start **and** end with the punch line and the story then appears in the middle. An old army instruction technique is "First tell 'em what you are going to tell' em: then, tell 'em and then tell them what you told 'em." My aim is not to instruct as in a textbook but to present my opinions as a framework for you to form yours. To some readers, it might sound like a textbook in places. To them, I ask for patience. Not everyone has learned the same things. It is helpful sometimes to make a point from its historical perspective and starting from basics can be more helpful than diving straight in at the deep end. The book is written primarily for younger readers (well, younger than me anyway) who may not be as aware of some of the basics as more seasoned readers may.

Good ideas are usually simple ones. Please do not judge too early what may appear simplistic, even naïve: some of my proposals may turn out to be quite advantageous in the end.

Beware the date

I wrote most of this book in 2004 and early 2005. You may be reading it much later. Please therefore make mental allowances for issues that were contemporary at that time but may now be just history to you. Mostly, I have tried to stick to timeless principles, but occasionally I cannot resist an anecdotal comment related to the times in which I lived and thus helped form my opinion.

Acknowledgements

My grateful thanks to Vyv Lewis who suggested important improvements in the early rough draught and the subsequent proofs. Also thanks to Julian Roskams of Etica Press for his late nights of editing, proofing and final design and to Rolf Harris for his kind Foreword and his numerous suggestions for improving some of my cumbersome sentences. One other VIP deserves special acknowledgement: my dearest, beautiful wife, Dee. She has been everything to me. I cannot praise her enough in every possible aspect. She is my Queen of Hearts and she alone makes me feel like her King. So, before I get too soppy, just take note that her presence and her influence flow through every vein of this book. Enough said.

Oh, except of course an acknowledgement to our three boys and their children who have quite unintentionally provided much of the source material for the development of the philosophies discussed herein.

Michael Kelly

Bray 2006

Contents

Foreword, *by Rolf Harris CBE* iii

Preface v

Note: Please pick any section you fancy – it is not necessary to start at the beginning but the order presented here is reasonably logical.

Who are we: what is the meaning of life? 1

A big subject condensed in just a few pages. Also covering religion and its alternatives. Is there a *right* belief? Is religion necessary? What is our purpose in life and what does it mean?

Islam and terrorism 11

Terrorism is a major threat. Most terrorists today are Islamic. Fires are fuelled by lack of understanding – by us. The West has asked for trouble and got it. What should we do about it?

Politics – the basics 18

Opinions on some of the fundamentals of politics including examples of how they work (or not) in practice.
Why should you be interested in Politics?

Understanding people and yourself 31

We all interact with people and need to have some idea as to what sort of person we are, as well as other person. What type are you?

The general theory of relativity and happiness 37

Being happy does not need material wealth. There is a knack to it and this section explains what it is, and why a hard early life can be lucky later.

Life planning and problem solving 41

Fail to plan and you plan to fail. How do you plan? How do your solve any problem? How do you weave a key ambition into a busy day-to-day life? Budgeting: Who is Mr Micawber and why is he important? Why is happiness a positive cash flow?

Education 49

If you think education is expensive, try ignorance! The more you know, the more content you will be. What are you best at?

Are you an entrepreneur? 53

Do you have what it takes to be a business leader? Would you like to promote yourself to Chairman of the Board?

Running a business 57

What do you need to do to run a successful business? See a list of do's and don'ts drawn up over many years of direct experience.

Investments, finance and mortgages 60

Money makes money. A short summary of the key principles of both investing and borrowing. How could you make money out of rented property?

Horoscopes, intuition and superstition 74

Do horoscopes really work? What is intuition? Should you be superstitious? What is wisdom? How do you get it? Why is it so important?

Medicine and psychiatry 78

How to get better without medicine. How to prolong life.

"Nothing in life is to be feared. It is only to be understood".

Marie Curie

"We make a living by what we get, but we make a life by what we give".

Winston Churchill.

"People spend a lifetime searching for happiness; looking for peace. They chase idle dreams, addictions, religions, even other people, hoping to fill the emptiness that plagues them. The irony is the only place they ever needed to search was within."

Romana L. Anderson

I Cannot Teach You

I cannot teach you, though the years
Have led me farther on
Along the path of life than you
In your short span have gone.
I can but lead you to the threshold
Of your thinking mind
And leave you there to search the worth
Of such as you may find.
I can but point the way, then you
Must travel your road alone;
The crossroads you will meet will not be
Those I have known...
The rest is up to you,
The choice is yours to make -
And I can only pray that 'tis
The right road you will take.

Helen Lowrie Marshall

Nothing lives forever yet life continues forever.

Michael Kelly

Life's a bitch and then you die.

Woody Allen

Dedicated to my grandchildren
some who are just glints in their grandfather's eye

Who are we: what is the meaning of life?

Everyone reaches an age when their personal curiosity about the meaning of life becomes more relevant to their lives, and their conscience starts to press for some serious answers.

My aim in this scene setter is to show how I initially looked at life and made my own conclusions as to the purpose of life. This inevitably leads to the question of religion and hopefully prompts you into coming to some conclusions yourself – not necessarily the same conclusions as mine. It is of course a huge, diverse subject, and can be controversial. Nevertheless, I have attempted to condense some big thoughts into just a few pages: it's worth persisting if only to firm up your own views.

Bill Bryson wrote in his magnificent work *A Short History of Nearly Everything* that we are extremely lucky to be *us*. In short, he said that we consist of some trillions of atoms that have somehow assembled in an intricate and obliging manner for a brief moment of time to become *us*. They then engage in numerous co-operative efforts simply to keep us *existing*, albeit for a mere 650,000 hours which is an infinitesimal fraction in the infinite life span of the mindless atom. They then drift apart to become something totally different.

He probably said it better than I remember, but that was the gist of it. In summary, we are merely a tiny, passing moment in the eternal life of a conglomeration of atoms.

Look at us on the macro scale – the human race. Physically we are really quite weird-looking animals: a bizarre, chemical potpourri of skin and bone containing a hodgepodge of highly complex organs, all made up of atoms. Half of our four prescribed limbs enable a primitive form of ambulation, albeit not as sophisticated as some of our more animal-like competitors. We have also been conveniently supplied with various orifices for varying purposes.

We are totally and absolutely dependent on our environment for survival. We have to take in and distill oxygen from our atmosphere every few seconds and would die within minutes if denied this vital process of respiration. To live out our average lifespan we regularly need to consume food and liquid by mouth, most of which reappears a little later from a couple more orifices, the only observable difference being a distinct change of colour and smell.

Our bodies miraculously extract and convert all the chemicals we need for survival just from what we push down our gullets. Such fodder was itself once as alive as we are, if you accept plants and fruit as living organisms, as well as all the other wildlife that we slaughter for their life-sustaining flesh. Apart from water and oxygen, un-alive items, such elements as earth or sand, have little part to play in this daily ritual apart from occasionally being catalytic. In essence, living beings need to devour other living things in order to stay alive.

The result is a living entity that can move about and reproduce, and be aware of itself. It seems that all living organisms exist simply to eat each other (albeit seldom the same genus) and to reproduce more of the same. There appears to be no other purpose in life other than sustaining life itself. All living things have adapted to exploit planet Earth's specific supplies and to recycle their waste products to assist in further production of other types of life. They then themselves recycle and eventually all life's sustenance moves round in a big organic circle: we probably eat a part of what was once our ancestors.

That the body can perform this extraordinary miracle of *existing* and reproducing is amazing enough, but why it evolved the way it has, what started it off and for what purpose, remain questions whose answers are as elusive today as they have ever been. We can but surmise.

We can trace our physical characteristics a very long way back. Fishes and monkeys apparently feature in our distant ancestry, which is probably why we are neutrally buoyant in water and some of us do look a bit ape-like. The urge to eat is a primitive but clearly vital instinct, and the search for evermore easily obtainable food is our principle daily objective, although camouflaged today in terms such as "earning a living".

Small insects can survive an even wackier life, adapting their strange physical bodies to suit specific lifestyles with remarkable variation – from slithery things with no limbs to crawly things with hundreds of limbs. They adapt feeding and reproductive habits to survive in the most extraordinary and, to us, hostile environments, ranging from very deep oceans to freezing, barren landscapes to near molten larvae. We still eat some of them and they would certainly eat us, given the chance.

Even more remarkable than some of the estimated 40 million or more species of animals and insects is at the micro-biological level – viruses and bacteria. They too have a sort of life by feeding off a host – usually us! These microscopic organisms can be deadly to beings that are trillions of times bigger. Viruses are very small micro-organisms that enter the cells of a host to replicate the cell. They are actually intercellular parasites. Bacteria are much larger and can replicate at the rate of hundreds in less time than our Earth takes to revolve once. Some are good bacteria as they attack even nastier ones on our behalf. Most are best avoided.

But we humans are special, because we have developed what we optimistically call *minds* to a relatively advanced degree. We are supposed to be the brainiest organism on the planet, which is why we have lapsed a bit in the physical department compared with other stronger, faster, bigger animals. But with our unique capacity for intelligent thinking, we can hopefully outsmart them in the ongoing competition for daily victuals.

We can also uniquely communicate with each other using speech and writing. There are some other animals with primitive social interaction abilities like grunting, chirping and barking but we *homo sapiens* are the real masters of thinking and then exchanging these thoughts with our colleagues. But even this extraordinary ability is limited. At the last count there were over 6,000 known languages used on Earth. The written formats and myriads of dialects are extremely diverse and derive from widely different histories.

Even using the richest of language, we can never fully communicate our real thoughts with absolute accuracy. Mind reading does not yet exist. We can only hope to give a broad hint as to our more profound feelings: sometimes we might wish to hide our true thoughts anyway. We have to resort to poetry, music and other artistic expressions to impart more complex thought processes, but such arts are always open to personal interpretation. In short, mutual communication remains imperfect. Consequently, there remains much misunderstanding in the world.

We have developed physical senses of pleasure and pain primarily to facilitate survival. *Pain* keeps us out of many life-threatening situations by warning us. Pleasure in eating urges survival: perversely, pleasure in killing ensures we know what we have to do to get our food. Pleasure in reproduction ensures we generate offspring to keep the whole cycle going. Mutual desire for suckling at the breast ensures that early offspring are fed by instinct.

Once we have passed our reproductive age, nature has decreed we have done our job and we now have to die. Our bodies cease aspiration and consumption but, by now, we have hopefully passed on the baton of life to the next generation who breathe on in our place. It seems that the whole purpose of life is life itself. Nothing lives forever yet life continues forever: and not just us – this applies to almost every animate entity on the planet. Over eons, natural selection ensures the weaker species fade away and the strong become stronger.

Our physical bodies take turns as life's guardians. Their purpose is to survive for sufficiently long to enable life to continue in new bodies. The egg seems more important than the chicken. We are certainly aware of our short temporary existence. We also have a handful of senses to interact with the world's other live beings, and we can reason with our minds. We can also pass on acquired knowledge to our children – if they ever listen.

We all need to *optimise* our personal security in order to stay alive for as long as possible by ensuring all threats to survival are minimised, and the arrangements for the provision of food and water are maximised. In the meantime we stay alive for as long as possible and hope to enjoy what pleasures we can. As *thinking* animals, this inexorably leads to a quest for *power*. The human race particularly possesses this compulsion to acquire influence and power, derived over many millennia from Darwinian-style selective breeding. This very basic urge for security by dominance also leads to fundamental inequality and much friction as a result. It certainly causes many world-class rows to say the least, and war is the ultimate result – even though the planet can more than adequately support all its inhabitants with plenty to spare, if ever we all acted sensibly. Human beings are certainly not equal.

So if humans are diverse, we survive on an even more diverse world of fellow creatures. That we survive at all is the result of an amazing set of cosmic co-incidences. The right-sized planet with the right sort and quantity of water and mineral resource: also just the right type and amount of atmosphere: and the right range of temperature variation, which is a tiny, miniscule span of hot and cold compared with those observed elsewhere in the universe. Although we evolved specifically to exploit this extraordinary environment, it is fortuitous that this mixture came together at the right time, as without it there could be no form of life at all as we know it. We probably evolved more by luck than by intelligent design.

After observing all this wondrous, miscellany of life for just a few decades or so, most people come to one of two main conclusions:

1. We might be part of **a** God's great plan in which we are personally loved and watched over by Him. Our lives are ordained and we have a greater purpose, although we are not permitted to know exactly what it is, only guess. Consequently we give thanks to this Deity and perform life's work as His (or possibly Her) servant and interpret and follow His rules as best we can. We might call this a religious process. We have to accept that while nothing is provable, only *faith* is required to accept this as true, although different societies seem to favour different faiths.
2. Alternatively, we might ignore *faith* as a factor and believe only in what we actually observe and analyse directly. Sadly, the logical conclusion of scientific method so far is that there is no detectable deity. There is no glorious happy-ever-after heaven, nor even hell, which might have been more suitable for some people I know. Eventually we all die and that is it – job done – no afterlife – just ashes to ashes. We must make the best of it while we are alive and then pass on that baton of life to our children.

   Some of us might not want to think this way, and many readers may find this idea offensive let alone depressing. I would love to have discovered that I am much more important to a God, and to actually feature in His diary. Disappointingly, it seems to me I am simply one of many lowly egg carriers for just a short while: then I am simply discarded. It is easy to see why many people prefer the easier option of a religious *faith*.

Facts are a good deal easier to find and analyse these days using our advanced information technology than it was say 150 years ago. We benefit from masses of more freely available information – from radio,TV,

Internet, as well as traditional books and newspapers. There is no excuse today for not knowing what is going on in the world, even if some of the details may sometimes remain obscure.

But horror! Despite this enlightened age we still endure war and terrorism, pain and suffering, hunger and pestilence – even worse in some cases than it used to be. It is not as beautiful a world as we would love to think. It is certainly not a nice God's world. We still all seem to act like ignorant animals, fighting and bitching all the time. Why is this? Will it ever change?

I believe the blacker side of humanity arises because of our relentless, in-born quest for security and thence a need for power in order to consolidate any hard-won sanctuary. It is natural instinct for any animal, for we are little more than sophisticated animals that can talk, and we all have the same survival instinct. A lion would hardly make a friendly survival pact with an antelope – that is his food supply. Despite our supposed special expertise in *thinking* and an improving ability to live comfortable lives, we will always remain merely advanced animals, and the survival of the fittest remains a basic rule of life. We all need to be fit and we all have to fight for survival. It's actually natural.

Luckily, we humans appear to be best of all breeds: if anyone can improve the world's modus operandi, it is going to be us. It is not natural to annihilate our own species as long as we recognise that everyone is part of it. We do have a tendency to expel some groups – usually differentiated by colour, race or religion – from our class. We should go about preserving our lives in a much more civilised way. I think we are slowly moving in that direction but clearly a great deal remains to be done.

Religion has provided one limited answer to our predicament – although to some people it is considered to be more an impediment. Although I am a non-believer, I do recognise the needs, opinions and beliefs of others and would never be contemptuous of those who hold a sincere faith. ("Now that's what I call really pompous", says Dee.) Let me explain:

Religion

According to my Google research, there are currently some 19 major world religions, which are themselves divided into around 270 large religious groups and many smaller ones. For example, apparently some 34,000 separate worldwide Christian groups alone have been identified. And every one of them fosters a belief that their members tread the righteous path. Yet they cannot all be right.

In general, religion provides a simple system of beliefs and practices, which provides groups of like-thinking people with acceptable answers to the quest for the meaning of life. For many people it is an entirely satisfactory explanation to their lives and no further research is necessary. Others may turn to religion later in life after a personal tragedy to help ease their pain.

Most religions proscribe a reasonable and gratifying moral structure and a code for living which, in the main, aims at civilised co-existence – as long as you are in the same religion. Religion provides moral leadership and points its members in a clear direction: it also prevents us from worrying any more about the purpose of life – God is dealing with it, so just relax and follow the creed. Christians have their very own ten commandments, a reasonable set of social rules conducive to peaceful living. Islam has the far more comprehensive Qur'an (often spelt in English texts as Koran), which lays down not just a religious code but also an all-encompassing daily ritual.

In general, those who follow a religious life seem to be more contented and fulfilled. Their religion provides them with moral guidelines, goalposts and traffic lights. People come together and they have a purpose. Prayer rituals provide an agreeable mechanism to address earthly as well as heavenly desires. Praying also encourages thought and self-analysis. Confession rituals force us to express the errors of our ways and so understand them better. Most religions also provide a pleasing answer to the after-life. One can also sin and then ask for forgiveness afterwards. Very handy! Great things are promised in heaven although terrible tortures await the sinners in hell – so be a good boy, or else! Life and death has been planned out for you, the rules are clear and excessive curiosity is unnecessary, particularly for the poor and ignorant.

The rich and powerful have been accused of using religion to secure their personal positions: indeed the medieval popes, such as the Borgias, were themselves deeply implicated in self-promotion rather than spreading the word of God. It is true that if the working proletariat (the great majority) follow acceptable social laws then better order is maintained. Those lucky souls with possessions are then less likely to have them stolen, or be killed for them. Since the prosperous and educated minority had much more to lose, and they usually made the laws anyway, the religious connection and its primacy were well worth encouraging. Those who transgress are then guilty of failing God's original law, rather than just a rich man's law. God's blessing was indeed convenient if you were wealthy and powerful since it is far more difficult to argue against God, particularly since He was not around that often and so His laws were accepted as "gospel".

Karl Marx summed it up well with his oft-quoted phrase "Religion is the opium of the people". Keep the peasants happily engaged with religion to stop them revolting against their inequitable treatment. After all, we cannot all be rich. Someone has to do the dirty jobs. Religion is therefore comforting for both rich and poor, though for different reasons, and for many it provides pleasing answers to some of the difficult questions about life and the hereafter.

I do not mean to sound cynical. This book is after all about my opinion: I clearly cannot disguise my true beliefs, despite attempting to be as dispassionate as possible. Face it: life is not really that fair. Those who have gained sufficient worldly goods to be secure and comfortable would wish to praise the system that got them there and now keeps them there in comfort. Those with little security and few possessions might find blame for their plight on something or someone else. If people believe that by being good and law-abiding that they too can go to a wonderful heaven, albeit later on, there is less earthly reason to revolt against inequity.

Nevertheless, there have been revolutions. Both the French Revolution and the Russian Revolution were about the excesses of the well-fed, privileged rich and were prompted by the starving, wretched poor. There have been other revolutions: but they all seemed to blow over eventually, order was restored and normal life continued, possibly the better for any aims that were achieved. The public does not really relish being without any leader for long, whatever that leader's inclinations might be.

Religion is both a blessing and a curse. Many would blame religion for some of the more brutal human conflicts. It is not just Islam versus

Christianity: there remain Catholics versus Protestants in Northern Ireland, Christians versus Jews in Europe, Sikhs versus Hindu in Asia. And so it goes on. Mutual hatred prevails. Even we atheists and agnostics cannot avoid the impact religion has on our world.

Having a belief in something is, to many of us, better than no belief at all. I can accept that, although I just cannot bring myself to pray, or to acknowledge the existence of any caring deity, in whatever form. In the early years of science, difficult questions about the universe were simply answered with a theological "fact". As we have discovered more and more about ourselves with good science, so the religious component has diminished. Scientists have now worked out that the universe started from almost nothing 13.7 billion years ago in a "Big Bang". Before that point there was absolutely nothing –no time, no space.

I still find that a difficult concept, but I am convinced there will be a clearer scientific answer eventually and not a theological one. But it is not imminent. In the meantime, I personally feel that I must simply make the most of being alive – I will be a long time dead. The problems of the living can only be resolved with better mutual understanding, not war, and humanitarian effort should focus on that. George W Bush please take note.

Summary & conclusion

I personally do not believe that there is a deity of any sort who runs our daily lives and that my soul might end up in a heaven or hell. However, life is certainly astonishingly miraculous, yet still no one really has a definitive answer as to why we are here and just what started it all, apart from "God". Religion is the easy answer but only a stop-gap.

You may well form a conclusion different from mine. Religion is certainly of great benefit for a large number of the world's population and, although severe religious tensions exist, this is more down to misunderstandings rather than the religious creeds themselves. I would be fearful of the anarchic vacuum that would result if suddenly everyone agreed that there was no God at all. God forbid!

The practical application of my opinion about religion is simple: attend to your own life without expecting any divine guidance. Devise your own philosophy rather than fitting into a religious cult. It is possible to be a caring, helpful human being without a formal religious creed. Dee thinks that living a good life, caring for others, thoughtfulness and honesty is a religion itself. If things go wrong in your life (they always do) then solve the problem yourself in a material, practical way and expect no help from a God. If he was once alive, He probably died some 13.7 billion years ago. (Please don't hit me with a fatwa for saying that!)

If He is there, I am sure He would understand what I am saying. For me at any rate, just having faith is not persuasive enough and essentially that would have been His fault as my creator, not mine. Our natural survival instincts were of His making and surviving can be tough on the non-survivors as ultimately we eat each other.

In short, I am all for religion as long as everyone else but me follows it. I simply believe that the purpose of life – is life itself. My natural role is to pass on the baton of life. My soul then passes on to the next generation. Perhaps that is a less glamorous role than I would like, but at least I am a fairly useful little cog in the grand machinery of the mysterious universe. I will also live Dee's good and honest life as far as I can, and pass on a similar creed.

So, live as long as possible, be a good helpful person, have fun, be wary and have grandchildren!

Islam and terrorism

We live in the era of the religious fanatic. Since the 11th September 2001 attacks upon the World Trade Center towers in New York (now known as simply "9/11" as American's put the month first), security everywhere has become very serious. It is a sad discovery that, according to some experts, the largest majority of terrorists in the world today profess to be of the Islamic faith. It therefore seems logical for me to follow on from the last section on religion and to look at the very real risks of living with the prospects of being blown apart by an Islamic suicide bomber. It is a very worrying trend and clearly a vital threat to our way of life.

My aim here is to urge you to make an effort to understand the motives behind this current significant wave of Islamic terrorism. In summary, we have more or less asked for trouble and we are getting it, but too many people fail to understand or accept this fact. Some comment is required: this is my opinion.

Islam is the religion of the Muslim people. Although difficult to prove, some Islamic statistics show that it is practised by more people in the world than any other religion (if you ignore agnosticism). Christian statisticians might come to a different conclusion. Islam has many historic similarities with Christianity and its numerous, diverse sub-classes. Both religions follow one God, although the Islamic God apparently had no human form like Jesus. The founder was a prophet called Muhammad who lived in the 7th century. He promulgated his beliefs through a book called the Qur'an.

In simple terms, Islam is based on five pillars:

1. **Faith**: There is no true god except Allah, and Muhammad is the Messenger of Allah.
2. **Prayer**: Ritually performed five times daily from dawn to dusk.
3. **Charity**: A percentage (one fortieth each year) is taken from every kind of property to be given out to the poor to enable them meet their needs.
4. **The Fast**: All Muslims fast from dawn until sundown during the ninth Islamic month of Ramadan, abstaining from food, drink, and sexual relations with their spouses.
5. **Pilgrimage**: At least once in their lifetimes, Muslims must visit Mecca.

There is much more detail in it than that of course, but compared to our Church of England we get off very lightly indeed. By the way, a fortieth (2.5% pa) means £25 from every £1,000 of assets – every year: very generous.

Islam has survived successfully for well over a thousand years with hardly any change. In its earlier history, the Islamic world was actually more dominant than Christendom, both culturally and scientifically.

But, like communism, the Islamic creed requires that its beliefs must be followed by *everyone* – certainly everyone in a Muslim country – to achieve ultimate perfection. Infidels (unbelievers) must be converted – if necessary by threat of Jihad (Holy War) according to one interpretation of the Qur'an. While Christianity also required expansion, and missionaries were dispatched to convert the mainly pagan world, there was never any Christian compunction to proactively wage a holy religious war as there is required in some interpretations of Islam.

Even before the medieval ages, Islamic peoples were successfully invading and converting Europe. They had converted Turkey and were invading parts of Spain and Italy and threatening Northern Europe. As a parallel, remember that when America helped defend Vietnam in the 1960s it was primarily to prevent the so called "domino effect" of one country after another falling to what was seen as the scourge of communism. The medieval version of this domino theory could be described as the Crusades in which the Christian world was forced to wage war to defend itself against the perceived Islamic threat of world domination and to regain lost holy ground. Some might argue that the Crusades were the Christian defence against Islamic Imperialism. Historical facts are somewhat murky around this dark medieval period – although, I for one, would love to believe in Robin Hood!

Islam is a complex religion and the western world, particularly America, have never properly understood it. Frankly, I am *still* struggling to comprehend some of it, but I believe it is very important to be aware of the beliefs of those who are our potential enemy: and, just as vitally, to distinguish those who are actually our Islamic friends. Like the Bible, Islam's Qu'ran has many interpretations but in the main it adopts a peace-loving, anti-violence creed and this is the message accepted by most Muslims: this majority group, as I see it, is **not** our enemy. Indeed, their faith seems to be more strict and morally structured than Christianity has ever been, although (Dee reminds me) it does seem to treat women very unfairly.

Religion cannot be dissected and analysed as if it were a science because it is not based on logic, nor backed up by any solid scientific principles. Most religions were founded on the basis of *belief* and an ongoing *faith*: proofs of scientific rigour are therefore unnecessary and irrelevant. Many older religions evolved from superstitions and other occult phenomena. Faith requires a set of beliefs that are very personal and virtually unimpeachable. It is even considered socially unacceptable to question another's faith. Islamic faith goes even further by setting out a comprehensive lifestyle that is isolated from and largely unfettered by political structures.

A more sinister interpretation of the Qur'an by the various radical fundamentalist groups supports, indeed encourages, the ultimate in violence against all infidels – Jihad – and particularly against America: "death to the infidels" being a typical mantra. Suicide bombing is even justified by their somewhat stretched interpretation. Unfortunately, it only takes a few extreme terrorists to create major mayhem for many innocent, and probably uninformed, people. It is easy for such a terrorist to maim and kill extraordinary numbers of guiltless people since, for them, the countless human tragedies they generate are irrelevant: this is a Holy War supported by God – the highest authority. "Death is honourable" and all the dead will return to life once again and, if worthy, to more privileged lives. No logic, but strong *belief*.

Old-fashioned, formal, chivalrous warfare used to be *declared* first, and was principally a battle of one army against another and never deliberately waged against civilians, although that was not always the case. But terrorists want revenge and victory at *any cost* and nothing and no one is excluded from their extreme methodologies. It is the ultimate form of barbarism, it is very hard to defeat and there are no rules: just extreme, unadulterated hatred, encouraged, and permanently sealed in the soul of the terrorist by Allah himself and as such, non-negotiable. It is an act of faith and belief. To an outside observer it seems primitive, but there is more to it than that.

We Westerners might find the moral justification for this extreme thinking difficult to grasp. After all, we think we really are a nice bunch of people, wanting to be friends with everyone: why do they hate us so? But they do, and because of what *we* have done. Now the threats are real, we must make a serious attempt to become more familiar with the answer to this question, to understand Islam better and particularly the interpretation of its extremists who currently present very real threats to the Western world.

The Western concept of democracy sets out a national way of life for the country that has little connection with religion. All religions are allowed to practice their faith unhindered. The nation lays down the law through a freely-elected political executive. This model is the reverse of the Islamic perception where *religion,* not politics as we know it, exclusively sets the principle routine of daily life, beyond anything else, and nationhood is simply a question of where to live. All citizens of a Muslim country are expected to follow the Islamic creed without exception. It's all written in the Qur'an.

Muslims do not have a word for *democracy,* a word we often interchange with freedom. Muslims do not need democracy – they have Islam and Allah, who is great. Their clerics decide on the law by interpreting the holy Qur'an as laid down by Muhammad around 1,400 years ago and enshrined as "Sharia Law". There is no need to vote for a government since the only legislation they need is God's. This idea may seem to us to be somewhat out of date, but there it is. That's *faith.*

Islamic states are situated in, what is to them, holy ground. To see *infidels* trample all over their sacred territory is a major insult to Islam, particularly when they see the motivation for it is simply our greed for oil.

It was only from about the 18th century that the infidel Europeans and Americans started to triumph over the Muslims in terms of scientific progress, power and influence, given the initial commercial impetus we enjoyed from our industrial revolution. At the start of the 20th century, the West needed oil for their new automobiles and machinery: we discovered masses of it in Arabia – but this was mainly sacrosanct Muslim territory. Regardless of such sensitivities, we all piled in and tapped into the rich oil seams, attempting to placate and bamboozle the Arabs (perceived by Westerners as uneducated and uncivilised) by promising much but doing little in return. Great Britain and Europe were just as much to blame as America in our disgraceful exploitation of the Arabs and incidentally, our broken promises about the Palestinians which was part of the original oil deal. You have to be open-minded to accept our early duplicity in some Arab affairs, facts that have only recently become better known to Westerners.

To many Muslims, who felt themselves to be the sole custodians of God's truth, and indeed were commanded by Him to bring this truth to all infidels, it was humiliating to find themselves dominated by the these very same infidels. When Muslim visitors familiar with the strict, principled code of Islam, studied our Western society, America in particular, they found it to be degenerate, delinquent and decadent. To a devout Muslim "Freedom" in the West seemed to mean "Anything Goes". It was not a happy experience: eventually the humiliation of Islamic regimes by the West turned to Islamic contempt for the West.

It should be no surprise that the growing resentment of the fundamental element of Islam to this Western-led "travesty" would eventually snap their patience. It took a certain Osama Bin Laden to vocalise this resentment in the last decade, and then to put in hand a terrible and continuing revenge starting with the destruction of the twin World Trade Center towers in 2001. One of his particular demands was for the infidels to leave holy Islamic territory, as required by Islam. We did the opposite.

The response of the infidels, again led by America, was a pre-emptive strike on Iraq in 2003 – this was some 13 years after *Desert Storm* forced the invading Iraqis from Kuwait, another big oil producer. The more recent, well-publicised, aggressive and heavy-handed treatment of the Iraqis, particularly prisoners, led to an even more undesired result – a thousand more Osama Bin Laden look-alikes and an even greater security threat.

I am ashamed of the late 2004 disclosures about America's treatment of the Iraqi people, particularly when in the same breath they say they stand for truth and decency. They claim they stand for democracy, human rights and the proper use of the law and yet imprison, torture and deprive foreigners of basic legal rights. It has immeasurably damaged the reputation of America, tarnished her supporters such as Britain and set back the cause of peace 10 years. These appalling double standards, practised by the leading superpower, may well encourage other Western countries to relax their own moral standards. The American leadership have deliberately linked the Iraqi invasion with 9/11 – yet no such link has been proved. We in the West can no longer claim to hold the moral high ground.

America keeps referring to "Victory" in Iraq, as if it were a war against the Iraqi people rather than relieving them of a hated dictator. It really does seems like they hate all Muslims because of 9/11 – yet the Iraqis had nothing whatsoever to do with it. No wonder normal peace-loving Muslims are frustrated.

While I have not studied the historical events talked of here in detail, I have formed an opinion from what I observe and from the opinions of independent experts. In essence, misunderstanding other religions and other lifestyles is a definite health risk. Bombing innocent, angry foreigners, who *we* probably stirred up in the first place, is no way to win security, peace and friendship. Diplomacy must succeed in the end, but not the old-school-style diplomacy of subtle intrigue and secret deals, but a new style of openness and genuine, mutual understanding and respect: no more stitching up. Appeasement is not quite the right word – it smacks too much of surrender – but perhaps conciliation, or arbitration, is a better expression, with a strongly led, independent United Nations as the central mediator. The West must act decently if we expect others to treat us in the same way. So far, our record is poor, and the United Nations (and its leader) has been useless.

Killing people is the ultimate admission of ignorance. It is unnecessary if we all take more trouble to understand each other better and work for less inequality in the world. It is so easy to say ,of course, and it is an obvious social ambition, but it is so important to recognise that we *all*, including our perceived enemy, fundamentally crave *security*.

Summary

Who knows which side will win? Ironically, if freedom fails and terrorism triumphs the Muslim people will probably be the greater victims. But our futures are somewhat vulnerable too. So take terrorism seriously. Try to understand its reasons. Superpowers have seldom defeated terrorism: reason wins in the end, and the hated terrorist soon becomes the beloved ex-freedom-fighter and is made president, as in Cuba, Israel, South Africa ... it happens more often than you think. Some might say America's president (Bush the younger) is still a terrorist.

But we must act like the decent human beings we seem to demand others to be. We have to encourage our leaders to behave decently. We must use our democracy to vote out the few evil people on our side and expose them in the full glare of world publicity so we too can be seen to condemn such deplorable, arrogant acts perpetrated in the interests of oil and world domination.

For a Muslim to willingly send his daughter off to become a suicide bomber must mean he is more than a little upset with the status quo. Killing them in return proves nothing except that even today's so-called "civilised" society still uses grossly primitive methods to make its point, and it achieves nothing more than increased anger and worse results.

Islamic terrorism needs thought and talk to solve the issues, not bullets and bombs. We need to care more for others and to show that we care.

Politics – the basics

I have now had my go at religion, which should be a personal journey of discovery. Let me now propose some opinions about another polite conversational taboo, and also a personal journey: Politics. My aim is to alert you to my perception of the good and bad bits of politics in order to help you make your own judgment. More importantly, I hope to encourage you to take an interest in politics, as it is part of the machinery of day-to-day life.

In the United Kingdom, the central question for most of us boils down to a decision on who will get our vote at the periodic local and general elections. It is not as easy a decision as it might seem. It is an important decision, even if you might wonder what difference one little vote might make in the grand scheme of things.

Some other countries operate a very different political system to ours – our main criticism of theirs usually relating to corruption, human rights and freedom. Happily, we British live in a so-called *Democracy*. In strictness, it is a Representative Democracy, where we vote for a representative (a Member of Parliament) to speak for us. The MP is faced with the perpetual dilemma of either speaking for his constituents or from his own view, or just rigidly supporting his party's manifesto. Future votes depend on whether promises are ever delivered.

Democracy is not a perfect system but it certainly beats Dictatorship and Communism. Democratic theory is fine. You vote in a secret ballot for your MP at least every five years to ensure any rogues don't last too long should their true colours turn out to differ radically from those first proposed to the electorate. A free press ensures free comment, albeit seldom unbiased. Often, dishonest reporters and press barons print lies and rubbish, usually to boost circulation. But rather a free press than one censored by the government, as happens in a surprisingly large number of countries who have unpalatable "truths" to hide.

The current "first past the post" voting system in Britain does produce some anomalies. Currently, only about 60% of the electorate actually vote. Moreover, at the most recent election, not a single MP was elected by a majority of his electorate. This seems to mean that most people are now represented by MPs they did not vote for. There clearly needs to be either a system of proportional representation or compulsory voting – or both.

Despite the anomalies, our British constitution is world-renowned, although, unlike the USA's version that it resembles, it is not formally codified. It remains a role model for many younger nations striving for fairer government. One of the key principles is what is called the "Separation of Powers". A freely-elected government becomes the *Executive*, which actually runs the country, but laws are made though parliament (the *Legislature*); and a separately-appointed *Judiciary* decides on whether the law was genuinely broken and dishes out the punishment. This separation is designed to ensure that the government cannot arrest and punish people at whim, at least in theory: there are some occasional exceptions, but usually for a good reason. Separating these powers limits the likelihood of a dictatorship emerg-ing. Incidentally, the strength of the police and law courts does not necessarily imply a strong society: rather they highlight the size of its moral imperfections, so we should not be proud of the number of prisons that have to be built.

The whole system focuses on freedom for *every* citizen. It permits ordinary people to become magistrates and to form a jury in order to judge other people's guilt and in public courts so that justice can be *seen* to be done. Religious and racial tolerance is legally enforced. Despite the UK's class-ridden history, life today is largely egalitarian and *Class* now relates more to merit and job description, and no longer solely to birthrights. The old concept of a privileged and powerful aristocracy is now already an historic relic, although it still means something to those who aspire to social climbing. When today's tycoons wonder what else they could achieve, many yearn for the perceived trappings of the old aristocracy, and becoming a Lord is their "crowning" achievement.

Money of course still makes a difference, and huge estates can be passed down despite capital transfer tax. But being rich today, and all the material and social advantages which go with wealth, is a position open to all, provided you have the necessary skill, ambition and determination. Your parents can certainly assist and encourage you, and knowing the right people certainly helps: but no longer are positions obtained simply because of historical parental "rank".

As life-long participants in British democracy, we are so used to it that we seldom question its world-class effectiveness, and do not often credit the long, sometimes difficult history which has brought it to its sophisticated elegance today. It is indeed imperfect and mistakes will be made from time to time. The voting system is imperfect: it is not proportional and a large opinion swing is required to bring in new legislation, and there are some inevitable anomalies. However, you should be proud and consider yourself lucky to be born in Britain and to live under such a largely fair system. There are too many examples in the world of far worse regimes.

British history was not always a story of decency, morality and fairness. Now is not the time or place for a history lesson, but suffice it to say our country's history is littered with dishonourable acts and harsh treatment of its citizens and its enemies. The consequences of our treatment of the Irish, the Palestinians, Indian sub-continentals and so on has been mixed, to say the least. It is a big, interesting study and it is not always easy to get at the unbiased truth. But despite Britain's moral leadership today, we cannot be too smug about our past, for not all of it was carved with pride.

Left or right?

World-wide, politics is broadly polarised into two opposing philosophies, classed as the *Left* and the *Right*. The left wing consists of Socialists or Democrats; the right wing are Conservatives, Tories or Republicans. The more left or right you are, the more extreme your views. There are many different names for these political stances depending in which country you live. There are also centre parties, such as the Liberals, who claim to pick the best out of each side. In my experience, people often vote for centre parties because they cannot make up their mind, or dislike both the main parties for varying reasons. I believe that all parties have flaws and some have flawed leaders. But I also believe that a clear choice should be made based just as much on the fundamental philosophical differences, as on just the man of the moment.

Left-wing supporters are essentially idealists striving for more equality but not always accepting that in reality people will always be unequal. The further you move to the left, the nearer you approach communism. Left-wing leaders like to control your life, so laws are focused on the state licensing as much as possible, albeit in an honest attempt to legislate for fairness. State money tends to be thrown at social problems as a priority, and consequently taxes are higher.

Right-wingers, on the other hand, accept that everyone is different regardless of their pedigree and that a free market-based economy functions in the consumer's interests: let the people have more say in their lives, have more choice and more money in their pockets by lowering taxes. Capitalism ensures private capital is tapped and not state capital. Nationalised industries are wasteful and ineffective because there is no competitive pressure for efficiency and no incentivised leadership.

Conservatives say their policies result in a vibrant economy where people do not rely on the state for everything. A healthy economy ensures jobs for all and competition minimises consumer prices. Sometimes if one moves too far right, tolerance for the less fortunate or for those of a differing race or colour, weakens to a point of violence, as it did with the Nazis and the Fascists in the last World War. Moderate Conservatives claim to serve *all* the people no matter what their circumstances and they would maintain the various social services' safety nets in order to banish outright poverty and hardship. They would not hand over taxpayers' money quite so easily as the socialists and they expect people still to contribute *some* effort themselves rather than leaving everything to the "Nanny State".

There is an unacceptable face of capitalism. This can be illustrated by the extortionate salaries enjoyed by some "top" business leaders that are closer to legalised looting than to any fair economic justification. Ultra-high pension deals and other high remuneration reflects more the powerful negotiating position of a managing director than the altruism of the shareholders. Remuneration committees, consisting of board level executives, will always encourage high salaries as they themselves are evaluated by similar committees on other boards. Every director of a listed company has a vested interest in the continuation of this internationally-accepted world of mutual back-scratching which is sometimes based more on comparables than a fair cost-benefit analysis.

Fortunately, the majority of our business leaders **are** properly remunerated, some even under-remunerated. Without the skill, experience and commitment of these people, shareholders would be worse off, the tax collected for the state would be lower, and more employees would be without work. Some would argue that jobs are lost anyway in the interest of competitive efficiency and shareholders' return. In some cases, this is a reflection of the real world and employees must themselves remember that their skills need to be bartered too. There is no justification for retaining staff at any cost, as eventually **all** of them could be out of work if that policy is continued.

The cynical liberal would say that, with socialism, a *public* criminal exploits the working people whereas, under a right-wing system, it is the *private* criminal who exploits the people. I think the *centre parties* are needed to help pull people back from these extremist trends: they are a bit like religion – you may not believe in it, but religion is necessary if only to help define morality.

Upbringing can affect your views – a personal story

One's own personal political leanings often relate to upbringing and lifestyle. When I was a youngster in my school Army Cadet Force, I could not help but notice two distinct classes of people: Commissioned officers, who seemed special, dressed differently and lived in a more distinctive style; and everyone else – the rest – the *other ranks* as they were rather off-handedly labelled.

Officers smelt of cigars, had dinner in the evening, eating off bone china, drinking cocktails beforehand, wine during the meal and port to follow. *Other ranks* had dinner at lunchtime and queued up for a dollop of sausage and mash in a mess tin. Officers strolled into work in smart tailored uniforms and were respectfully saluted. Other ranks saluted every officer, wore shapeless, ill-fitting uniforms (which came in two sizes – *too big* and *too small*) and were bawled at by the sergeant-major: *other ranks* did all the work. *Other ranks* sweated – officers merely perspired. Officers gave orders, *other ranks* obeyed. Officers were paid more money, enjoyed more privileges and generally seemed to have a far better life in all respects than the *others*. Officers did not work in the physical sense – they thought and planned and took responsibility.

I had the choice of abhorring this seemingly inequitable set up or accepting it and choosing sides. I decided I wanted to be an *Officer,* or of that class. I was unlikely to enjoy life much by fighting it and unlikely to change it. The *other* ranks seemed to be perfectly happy with themselves and actually enjoyed great comradeship, and worried less – but I decided I did not want to be an *other rank*.

Life outside the army seemed to be similarly polarised. There were Directors, or *The Management*, and there were the *Staff* – the worker bees. Again, if you were the boss, you had access to all the privileges and advantages that life had to offer: if you were not in that lucky division, you missed out on the best bits. It seemed that the winner took it all, despite the additional burden of responsibility properly carried by them and the longer working hours often spilling over into home life. The worker bees were content to be led and not have to take risks. It seemed a good bargain to me.

How did one join this elite group? In the old days it was just a question of birth. The children of the privileged classes automatically inherited the same privilege and rank. Not so now. While it still helps to be born to a successful family where the necessary qualities are readily apparent, you first had to *want* to be successful. The process of actually getting there is partly down to innate ability but mostly ambition and drive – the basic attributes of the entrepreneur – which will be discussed in more detail later on. If you want to be a boss, you simply promote yourself. Not everyone has what it takes.

My mother knew what to do. I don't know how she knew. We came from a very normal working family, with nothing distinctive and certainly no inherited capital. But mother was determined that her son was going to Cambridge University and that he "become a success". When she discovered I had failed Latin at O level – then a prerequisite to Cambridge entry – she worked out that as an *army* entrant, Latin was excused. So I was packed off to join the army – as a potential officer of course! I was sent to Welbeck College; a pre-Sandhurst army sixth form college for alleged brainy types who were needed to lead the military's engineering corps.

I have to acknowledge my mother's remarkable foresight. It all worked out according to her grand plan. I duly went to Cambridge as a 2nd lieutenant and left the army after some 12 years of military service as a modest Captain. But by then, I was firmly attached to the officer's lifestyle.

As far as politics was concerned, officers usually voted Conservative. This is because the Conservatives, or the Tory party, more thoroughly recognised that ambition and entrepreneurship is a necessary part of economic progress. Tories understand market forces better than Labour – and the science of basic supply and demand: if you tinkered with market forces you usually ended up with the reverse of what was planned unless it was done very carefully. Labour always wanted to tinker because they refuse to accept that each person is different and they love *control*.

The lowest ranks often felt hard done by, and probably were. They voted Labour. This was usually because the Old Labour party was determined to level out society as they saw it, so those on the bottom rungs had nothing to lose: and the toffs would one day be brought down a peg or two. Labour wished to reform some of the less fair aspects of society: union power helped and was part of that process. So if you were a labourer, you usually voted Labour.

The old Labour party was unhappily rampant with extremists. Some of them had a big chip on their shoulder, possibly due to them or their family being treated unfairly at some time, but often envy and desire for retribution was stronger than their more honourable aspirations for sensible reform. Michael Foot was once the leader of the Labour party and I remember him saying on TV, sometime in the 1970s, that "no one should earn more than £5,000 a year". Given that £5,000 then is clearly worth much more today, it was more the fact that he though that a *cap* on earnings was necessary for social equality. I found that statement quite astounding, and fortunately most of the electorate at that time did too and the party was virtually unelectable. The Labour party 1983 manifesto, an avowedly left-wing programme, was described by one member as the longest suicide note in history, and produced Labour's worst election result in 40 years.

Clearly political issues are not as simple as that. Some successful capitalists vote Labour, although the reasons remain obscure. Years ago, Tory legislation was often seen as pro rich and anti poor – and the reverse applied to Labour. There is an element of truth in both these accusations. Fortunately most of the more serious anti-worker abuses have now been sorted out, and so has much of the abuse of union power.

But *New Labour* under Tony Blair is a different animal altogether.

The "New" Labour party

New Labour will be remembered in history for its blatant use of *spin* to gain and then regrettably to *abuse* power. *Spin* means all talk and no action. New Labour's acolytes "listened to the electorate" and simply promised to do what the majority wished. This turned out to be almost identical to the Conservative's vision. The Tories were in disarray at that time and they failed to differentiate themselves enough: *New Labour's* manifesto was voted in with a massive majority, yet Tony Blair seemed to be almost as right wing as his avowed hero, the great Margaret Thatcher.

But Blair's Government has set a new level of despair for those who yearn for truthful government. 60-odd stealth taxes introduced by the longest-serving Chancellor, Gordon Brown, have also set new standards of subterfuge in order to rip out ever more dosh from the unsuspecting taxpayer, at the same time spinning the tale that there has been "no rise in [basic rate] income tax". The *rate* has not risen but the total tax and National Insurance actually *paid* certainly has.

The annual additional state take of some £6 billion in tax *every year* from previously tax-exempt pension funds represents another con for the working population – name any average worker and pension holder who is really aware of the true nature of the statement "withholding tax on dividends is no longer being eligible for refund". Sounds so innocent, doesn't it? It isn't!

This type of government cannot last, but they are even tinkering at the very core of our democracy in order to stay in power, and trying to blur the crucial *separation of powers* concept so fundamental to our constitution. Be very careful indeed when you vote: *New Labour* is not a proper left-wing government: it is a power-crazed party which really thinks like *Old Labour* but which dare not say so publicly for it would be unelectable, as was poor Mr Foot.

I mentioned earlier the left's propensity to tinker with market forces and often to produce the opposite effect of what they wish for. A classic example of this in practice was Chancellor Gordon Brown's action to tax pension fund dividends in 1998 as mentioned above. This had the effect of discouraging pension funds to invest in shares: other investments such as gilts and property escaped being tax-penalised. Pension funds used to invest an enormous amount of money in the stock market, but their appetite for equities was somewhat dulled by this new tax, therefore creating less demand for equities. Consequently, share values fell, or at least rose less than normal – supply and demand affects share prices very directly. Resulting lower share prices reduced the overall investment return on pension funds still further. What a debacle! Some civil servant probably told Gordon that the state could raise £6 billion from pensions without affecting basic rate income tax: the Chancellor grabs the chance, regardless of the effect on market forces, and almost ruins the pensions industry.

Another example of a lack of understanding of market forces is in the regulation of financial products. When the stock market fell, the regulator reckoned that insurance companies had insufficient liquidity and so they were obliged to *sell* shares and buy government stock. The result – a further fall in the market, asset values dropped even further and policy holders suffered once again from basic regulatory incompetence. The time to buy shares is in gloom not boom – the regulator is insisting on the reverse. It turns me grey with frustration (good excuse, eh?!). When will they understand market forces? Aaaagh!

People really are different

Many honest-thinking youngsters often start out with political views left of centre: they are naturally concerned for what appears to be an unfair distribution of wealth. Well, it sounds so innocently fair and right and proper to think this way. (I remember the youthful but cynical definition of a communist as "a person with nothing who wishes to share it with everybody".) As one gets older and more observant, the vast differences in people's talents, attributes and, more importantly, ambition is clearly so large that full-on Marxist-style egalitarianism, despite its good intentions, is just impossible in the longer term.

Think on this. Suppose that one day everyone's personal wealth was all redistributed so that everyone in the country over the age of, say, 18 abruptly received an identical lump sum. Everyone then starts off with exactly the same amount of money. Interestingly, inside a year or so, most of the same people would have regained their original wealth by sheer enterprise. The other part would have simply spent it and ended up in their original state too. Wealth would soon be re-redistributed back to where it was originally – and quite quickly too. Look at the stories of the big pools and lottery winners for evidence of the "spend spend spend" culture.

You may doubt this until you have met more people and have investigated why some people are wealthy whereas others are destined to remain poor. It is partly down to different personal talents, or the lack of, and partly due to personal ambition. People are very different; some are born more able than others, however unfair that may seem.

No longer can one blame the class system as divisive. Sadly, the very left wing are still more obsessed by class than any aristocrat would be. Today, everyone enjoys an equal chance of being wealthy: interestingly most millionaires come from poor backgrounds, often with limited education, but their hunger for success gears up their drive and determination. Others are quite content to live off the state – this means living off the working taxpayers who supply the government's loot!

No one has any real excuse to be hungry in today's nanny welfare state. If you still end up destitute, you may well have bought it on yourself. I am not being heartless – we have all heard the sad stories of those who fell through the net – I am simply summarising my personal observations. This does not mean these unfortunate people should be excluded from state assistance or care. But conversely, anyone who has made anything of themselves today deserves praise not criticism, for that person supports the less well off with a significantly higher tax payment, tax on earnings, tax on capital profits, tax on investments, tax on assets passed over on death, and value added tax (VAT) on what is spent. It's about time the successful producers were praised and the lazy takers given a kick up the arse.

Even New Labour recognises that the country needs entrepreneurs, more so now than at any time in history, because there are fewer and fewer workers having to support more and more people on state pensions or on welfare benefits. Ironically, it has been shown that higher tax *rates* often reduce the total tax take. If the top level of tax is too high, it becomes a disincentive for the go-getters to bother go-getting any more, and so the country and its citizens fail to achieve their full potential.

Another anomaly, which annoys me, is the need for higher rate tax bands. It does seem fair to me that, after initial allowances, if you double your income, you should pay double the amount of tax. But, for some mysterious reason, higher earners are not only expected to pay more tax, but also at a higher *rate*, so they pay much more than double. If the tax rate band increases from say 20% normal to a top band of 40% –

that's *quadruple* the amount of tax for the higher earner, not just double. That strikes me as an envy tax and a disincentive to achieve more. It is too facile to claim that higher earners can afford it.

Another annoyance on the same theme is council tax. Those with bigger houses pay more council tax. Why? This tax, unlike income tax, supports local expenditure such as schools, police and rubbish collection. Bigger house owners do not necessarily have more children – often the opposite – or bin more rubbish, or have a greater need for police or fire services, usually the reverse. So why do they have to pay more? Because, the councillors say, they can afford it. Michael Foot still lives on in some souls.

Margaret Thatcher was voted from office over her policy to resolve this inequity. She introduced the Community Charge (dubbed the "Poll Tax") which was a far fairer system than the old rates system. Her plan was that payments were to be based on the number of people living in a house rather than just the house value. Council services are based on the number of users of its services and have nothing to do with house values.

However, this meant that wealthy house owners with few occupants would now have their previous local council bills significantly reduced, whereas many council house tenants with legions of live-in family members would now be paying per head and clearly paid much more than before. It was the changeover that brought so much discontent, not the policy. Despite the clear, basic fairness of the Community Charge, there were such outcries and occasional vicious revolts ("Forcing the poor to subsidise the rich") that Maggie was accused of "not listening to the public conscience" and eventually one of the finest leaders of this country was discarded by her own party. Disgraceful!

The basic cause was socialist politics, which decreed that the rich should pay for almost everything. One Labour Chancellor (Dennis Healey, I recall) actually proposed a wealth tax, saying he was "...determined to squeeze the rich until the pips squeaked". Michael Foot again. No perception of market forces or any understanding why the rich are needed to pay for and employ the poor. In those days higher rate tax was 98%! Yes – unbelievable, but that was Old Labour – the same as New Labour in disguise.

I guess my voting intentions are pretty clear by now. Like religion, politics can be an emotive subject, but it should not be one to avoid. Politics is a big issue: the people we vote into power represent us. Democratic methods are blunt, in that you might well have a politician in power who did not get your personal vote. However, you at least have the freedom to talk your friends around to your point of view for next time: this is how politics should work. Be open and do not feel there is a taboo about talking about it. Discuss things. Get involved.

No political system is entirely fair. Power tends to corrupt; absolute power corrupts absolutely. Sadly, the world is full of corruption and exploitation. Often such unscrupulousness can camouflage the real issues. For example, President Robert Mugabe (Zimbabwe, formally Rhodesia) is despised by the West for his allegedly shady methods for taking back land previously taken from the indigenous black population.

However, British-born Cecil Rhodes (1853–1902), who made a fortune from mining diamonds in the area and gave his name to Rhodesia, as Zimbabwe was called from1893 to 1980, joined up with some other British cronies to do the original mischief. Together, in the name of Britain, they took over the country, cheating and then sweeping aside the king and his black subjects, who had been there for over a thousand years before. In short, we behaved disgracefully in the first place by unfairly exploiting the blacks: it is no wonder some of them are feeling bitter. But all one reads about are the excesses of Mugabe, seldom the historic sins of Great Britain. There are always more sides to a story than are published in the newspapers and it can take some effort to unravel the truth. As I write today, the BBC website is not a bad place to start, but do not believe all you read: persevere and dig deeper; the results are often surprising.

Incidentally, please note that the "government" does not pay for anything: it is the taxpayers who actually pay – the government only decides who pays and gets paid. So let's not talk of government funding – there isn't any – it all comes from you and me – the taxpayer. Many people think that if the state pays then it's free. Not so! The state means you. That is why it is vital to choose who you want in charge of spending a substantial chunk of your hard-earned money.

Summary

Great Britain Ltd is like **your** club. It is a great club. You may not like the current management committee, but you still need to follow club rules and pay the club subscription to enjoy the benefits. Get involved in the club activities. You will get a chance of changing the management periodically, or even becoming the management. If, on balance, you still really do not like what you get – emigrate and join another club!

I have written about some examples of politics in action from my own perspective to demonstrate that democracy in action has its faults. New Labour in particular is (in my opinion) a dangerous "spin and stealth" party. In short, you must perform some stringent analysis before you decide to support them.

Remember that not all you read in the so-called free press is true. You need to dig quite aggressively to discover the reality. Genuinely independent magazines are hard to find. *The Week* is excellent and Auntie BBC tries hard to be independent and publishes many important stories in great depth on its website.

Keep your mind open. Talk about politics but listen to and respect the views of others – sometimes you may change yours.

Understanding people and yourself

We interact with other people almost every day. I would like to alert you to some of the pitfalls when attempting to understand your fellow humans and, not least, yourself.

I have had two pieces of luck to assist me in understanding myself and others. Firstly, the first 10 years of my life were spent without a father: I was what was called a "war baby". In fact, I only met my real father once before he died. Consequently, I had no live-in image to help me shape my budding temperament and I had to resolve my developing nature for myself by observing numerous other alternative father images instead. While this might have delayed my early emotional development, it enabled me to be more selective when putting the finishing touches to my persona. I could pick and choose the more desirable characteristics when I was more physically mature.

The second lucky break was in bringing up stepchildren as well as my own son. This illustrated to me very clearly the overwhelming influence of *nature* on character types rather than *nurture*. In other words, it became obvious, over years of observation, that upbringing, no matter how thoughtfully and lovingly deployed, cannot change a basic character, which is set and locked at birth from inherited genes.

Dee attended a sociology course many years ago. I could not wait to read her course notes and found myself as absorbed in the subject as she was. One of the areas discussed was the apparent dichotomy of whether our basic nature was more influenced by "socialisation" (environmental influences such as parental upbringing) or by inherited characteristics. While the academic debate still rages on, to me the answer can be explained with a simple analogy.

Heredity certainly maps out one's physical characteristics. Your eye colour, hair colour, bone structure and general genetic makeup clearly have nothing to do with your environment. Our body arrives pre-equipped with a set of components extracted from our parent's storehouse: their supplies were similarly derived from their ancestors. By mixing *two* parent's components, the resultant child will possess a new combined set, developed over many thousands – probably millions – of years, through natural selection. Not every little component is passed on, and sometimes a few nuts and bolts get lost on the way. Sometimes more of one parent's chromosomes than the other are handed down. Heredity remains a lottery.

Socialisation through environmental influences is the process by which these specific components are assembled and switched on. Think of the body as a robot to be assembled from the box of items supplied at birth. There is no blueprint. The bits are gradually soldered together as the "robot" grows up, and eventually it will walk and talk in strict accordance with the components supplied. But no amount of knob-twiddling thereafter will enable you to change the fundamentals. Once you are conceived, that's it – no more components. This does not just affect our appearance, but our capacity to think, to remember, to deploy all our senses, instincts and feelings. No amount of upbringing can create a musician or a scientist unless the basic ingredients were there in the first place. You cannot make a good curry without the right spices, regardless of how skilled the cook.

While basic character and appearance is set by birth, environmental influences put those components together and make them work. You can still abuse a good set of inherited characteristics by being badly brought up. For example, you may have inherited all the attributes to become a great sportsman, but if you have been encouraged to be lazy, or made to focus on something very different, you may never even know your full potential. Conversely, you cannot force someone to be highly academic if they don't have the necessary brain cells. Your beliefs and your personality can be strongly influenced by your parents and your peers but your basic character cannot.

A prince and a pauper can be exchanged at birth and given the appropriate upbringing of their mistaken positions: the original Pauper may well display all the superficial trappings of royalty, but he may never display the inspirational gravitas and leadership qualities possessed by the hereditary prince, which would have been shaped over centuries of selective breeding. This may be a facile example, but it embellishes the point that you cannot make a silk purse from a sow's ear.

I think it is essential to make an inventory of your own basic components. Similarly, parents should check out their offspring too and then relate their ambitions to what is possible, given what is there. Once it is clear what type of apparatus and ingredients have been inherited, then is the time to start testing each in-born attribute and its capacity until you know your strengths and weaknesses. Only then can you assess the opportunities open to you and any shortcomings preventing you achieving them.

Motivation

We always act for a reason. It might be a stupid reason, but there is always a pay-off for whatever we do, whether it is good or bad. If we find ourselves acting in a way that we discover is causing us problems (eg smoking, dinking or eating to excess) we must find the real motivation and analyse that, rather than making a series of excuses or raising a smoke screen. Easy to say, yes, but identifying your personal motivation and the motivation in others is probably the best key to understanding human nature.

Attitudes and personality types

Basic attitudes are definitely influenced by upbringing. For example, parents who do not encourage a questioning curiosity in their children, or basic literacy, will usually end up with a dull child, unless the inherited characteristics are strong enough to push through without parental encouragement. A home without basic good manners may result in a child who is thoughtless and self-centered despite his or her genes. But sometimes these shortcomings can be corrected later in life, given that the basic ingredients still exist, the shortcomings have been recognised and the will to learn has survived. For example, vocal dialects are inevitably derived from upbringing. While there is nothing wrong with a charming dialect, poor pronunciation and badly constructed sentences can seriously reduce mutual understanding. With some personal effort, such bad habits *can* be changed for the better.

Bringing up children can be quite fraught (see later sections). The difference between producing a sullen, rebellious and even criminal youngster on the one hand, or one with self-disciplined determination to succeed on the other, can often result from a small difference of emphasis. Given the basic ingredients, upbringing can have a major influence on the resultant personality though not on the character.

With a bit of experience and careful observation, it is possible to identify the key elements in people of both upbringing and hereditary characteristics. There are good signs (meeting of eyes, good humour, enthusiasm) and bad signs (shifty look, bad temper, negative outlook). You need wisdom to tell the more subtle differences. There are many books and websites that sub-divide personal traits into several neat boxes and then sum up your personality and what job you would suit depending on ticked boxes. Over simple perhaps, but helpful nevertheless.

Jung was one of the earliest psychologists to attempt to make a science of Personality. For example, he postulated that there were two basic types – the Extroverts (expressive people) and the Introvert (reserved people). Extroverts talk more, take risks, like socialising and seem very positive. But they listen less, and hence learn less. Introverts sit back, say less but observe more and are more likely to come up with a practical brainwave. Reserved people can enjoy being solitary whereas expressive people get bored more easily.

In my experience, people can never be so easily sub-divided and most have combinations of each. Here are some simple examples from a social setting.

1. Someone who constantly talks of his or her achievements and is uninterested in yours is clearly self-centered. However, they may have been unappreciated as a child, yet actually have genuine talents. Do not immediately write them off as bores: question their upbringing. This type of person usually enjoys the interest that you take in them and will be eager to talk. They will think of you as a good companion because you have demonstrated an awareness in them. Of course, they might still turn out to be bores.
2. A quiet person who seems dull and uninterested in talking could be a thinking introvert who may well have some interesting and unusual views if you take the trouble to ask. They may end up being fascinating, with some atypical but excellent ideas.
3. A salesman will often "network" and use any social occasion to push his product. There is no harm in that in itself (it may be an excellent product) although it is bad manners if it is prolonged: but

recognise that his positive-sounding conversation may well be biased. He or she may be asking questions not out of genuine interest in you, but as a sales ploy to pinpoint as a possible prospect.

4. Someone who is obviously a bit tipsy will never make any sense, so avoid forming opinions at this time, other than that he might have a serious drinking habit if it repeats. It does not necessarily mean you have met a sad alcoholic – it could just mean someone has just temporarily succumbed to excess to celebrate a succ-ess. However, having observed the negative effect his state has on the opinions of those around him, remember to avoid being drunk yourself as you might be tarred with the same brush.

These uncomplicated examples could go on and on. The pothole I am trying to identify here is the danger of *pre-judging* people. You cannot escape the necessity of eventually forming an accurate opinion of everyone with whom you interact in the longer term. So keep an open mind about people after the first meeting. Often their true natures turn out to be quite different after you have got to know them better. The more you ask people about themselves, the more you learn and the quicker and more practiced you become at summing people up.

Summary

Judging people too early on invariably produces a wrong assessment. After over 50 years of observing people, I have begun to value just a few desirable characteristics that are mainly related to honesty and integrity. Integrity means you are genuinely concerned that what you say you will do, you will actually do. It takes more than a few meetings to discern these straightforward attributes, but once established, these people often become firm friends.

On the other hand, those who show excessive economy with truth and seldom deliver their promises are likely to be fickle on just about everything else. Avoid them.

I still make mistakes about people today – nobody is perfect, except you-know-who – she is, of course. However, the mistakes are usually about people who I thought at first were straight but who eventually proved otherwise, rather than the other way round. They were perhaps more subtle in hiding the truth. So be wary. But be interested. We all need other people, and understanding them better is advantageous; ignoring them or misunderstanding them can be a dangerous mistake. Note particularly the later section on Marriage in which a proposed practical list of criteria is offered as an aide-memoire.

Finally, remember you cannot change the basic characteristics that you inherited but you can exploit the good ones with the right environmental encouragement and, hopefully, dim the significance of any bad genes that might be lurking in the machinery. Attempt to identify the motivation behind people's actions to understand them and yourself better.

The general theory of relativity and happiness

No, not Einstein's e = mc^2 and all that physics. I mean Kelly's homegrown theory of happiness being *relative* not *absolute*. My objective here is to convince you that happiness can be an acquired skill and is independent of environmental factors and personal wealth.

Imagine for a moment an average, young married couple with one small son living on a low-cost housing estate. They have saved up for two years to put the deposit down on their first new car. The excitement builds as the delivery day arrives and the husband negotiates a day off work. The gleaming machine duly arrives and it looks just wonderful. It is a beautiful shiny, metallic 'moondust silver' Ford Ka, managing over 40 miles to the gallon and has a radio and cassette player. It cost just over £7,000 and they had persuaded the salesman to provide some extras for free: a bouquet of roses from the salesman adds to the thrill of the day.

They love it and name it VeroniKa: the whole family drives off to their in-laws to show it off. Photos are taken; other proud family members are taken out for a spin. They play the radio really loud. It is one of the happiest days of their lives.

Ten miles away, a wealthy businessman has had his secretary order his next executive car, a new Rolls Royce to complement his wife's Mercedes SL Sports which she changes every year. It's his third Roller. He has forgotten to tell his wife and casually mentions it over dinner. They agree to go for a drive when it arrives if he has the time.

The businessman obviously feels very happy about his new car too. But perhaps not with the same intensity as our poorer youngsters in the next village who really had to struggle to buy their new Ford. His Rolls cost 20 times as much as their little Veronika, and has every imaginable luxury. Nevertheless, his *elation* quotient, while very positive, is somewhat lower. What do we make of this?

Clearly happiness is a *relative* state and not an absolute one. It is unrelated to absolutes like money, position or status. It is a mental state of feeling good as opposed to feeling bad. It is a positive, happy state as opposed to a negative, sad state: both states hover around a neutral, normal level that is different for everyone. A starving Ethiopian may well obtain as much gratification from a crust of stale bread as a well-fed Englishman would from consuming a medium-rare steak.

The point is that happiness is an *inner contentment* and not an environment issue. It is in the mind and not just a physical feeling. It is relative only to your neutral state of mind wherever the body is situated. This means that you can find pleasure in almost any situation if you search for it.

I am personally delighted by this discovery. I think there is actually a knack in being happy. Life generally dishes up happy moments and bad moments in almost equal proportions. It just happens that way. My strategy is simple: search out and maximise the good parts of life and play down or ignore the bad bits, and then make a habit of it. It is almost as easy to be habitually miserable – I've met a few people like that. I recommend the former. However tough life may appear to be, there is always a sliver of good news somewhere to focus on. Relish it.

Dee & I often sing the Johnny Mercer song, which says it more memorably:

You have to – accentuate the Positive
Eliminate the Negative
Latch on – to the Affirmative
And don't mess with Mr In-Between.

Romana L Anderson also reflects my feelings in more poetic words, which I listed at the beginning of the book. To save you looking back, they were:

"People can spend a lifetime searching for happiness; looking for peace. They chase idle dreams, addictions, religions, even other people, hoping to fill the emptiness that plagues them. The irony is the only place they ever needed to search was within."

I must add a rider to this apparently simple technique of being happy. No one is happy all of the time. Nature has proscribed random and inevitable hazards to test us. While "being happy" is a short-term state, *contentment* is the desired longer-term feeling. Contentment means you are comfortable with your achievements. Setting yourself an achievable aim, and then achieving it provides the bedrock on which you can suffer occasional, rare bouts of unhappiness but never serious ones. Contentment is still an inner state of mind, but it needs more than just being positive to be sustained: it needs some sense of achievement as well. Achievement also facilitates confidence, which then improves the chances of contentment still further.

There are some negative longer-term mind states that can eat into this inner contentment. Envy is one. A sense of failure is another. There are others. You will know what they are if they affect you. Come to terms with them as quickly as possible and move on, or you will end up a perpetual misery.

The game of life

No matter how carefully you try to plan, there is always some unexpected surprise round the corner. Just when you thought you had understood a pattern, it suddenly changes. Not always, but occasionally, and usually when you least expect it.

Life can be like a daily game of poker. You never know what cards you will be dealt. Half the time you get a good hand, some useful high cards and some aces. But equally, and with statistical certainty, the other half of the time you are dealt a load of rubbish. Fortunately, real winners can still turn a bad hand to their advantage, whereas less skilled players can really mess up a lucky deal.

Therefore, it is the *play* that counts and not the cards you get. Play the game well regardless of the cards dealt, and you stand a better chance of staying ahead in the happiness stakes. In short, it is how you actually live your life regardless of your circumstances and those inevitable periods of bad luck, and it is the positive decisions you make day to day, that separate the seemingly lucky from the sad.

The advantage of a hard life

In the same vein, I remember meeting a famous comedian, who once used to live next door to us. A book written about him refers to his early life when he was being sexually abused by his father. It could have seriously disturbed a lesser man. But instead of crying over it and using it as an excuse for any bad happening, he simply put it behind him and became more determined that this early trauma would never adversely affect him. This positive attitude resulted in a remarkable career. His name – Billy Connolly.

On a recent first visit to India we, like most tourists, were appalled at the poverty. Yet most poor Indians had a ready smile and accepted their sad lot with abundant cheerfulness regardless. It was very refreshing to observe this positive outlook against desperate circumstances, and it underlined my point about happiness being relative. Of course not everyone was pleased with their position in life, and clearly the better off will always find it easier to find happiness. But a positive outlook helps all classes to find something to smile about.

I have also met people who blame their unhappy childhood for the paucity of their lives. I say to them, use your bad experiences to *strengthen* you for the future and do not dwell on a bad or miserable past. This philosophy is similar to performing a well-known engineering routine called *work hardening*. Take a piece of iron. Heat it to red, give it a good bashing with a hammer and then douse it in cold water – the result is a far tougher piece of metal. Some initial heat and hammering *can* be an advantage in life too.

Summary

Being happy is an acquired skill. It is an inner contentment, unconnected with status or wealth. It is a relative state of mind and not determined by absolute factors. The simple secret is to be positive and proactive about everything: identify the good, happy bits in your life, and then relish them. Accept that there will always be bad moments but these will pass and soon forgotten.

In the longer term, being content with one's achievements can gradually increase one's resistance to setbacks and the inevitable unhappy moments: these can then pass by more quickly and with lessening impact. Achievement gives you confidence. Identifying negative traits is important too, so they can be quickly excised.

Happiness is a gift of nature – but it must be seized or it might be lost in a sea of melancholy.

Life planning and problem solving

"The purpose of life is life with a purpose."

A key ingredient in Dee's and my business achievements was undoubtedly *good planning*, something I learnt initially in my 12 years with the army. I remember my old instructor's order "Fail to plan and you plan to fail".

This philosophy has also been crucial to us whenever life turns an unexpected corner, as it often has. Having a clear goal, and a good plan to get there, simply facilitates living, particularly when you have to make the occasional deviation to cope with the inevitable, unforeseen banana skins. At least you have a map.

Time is precious – and it is vital to handle it well. The following idea is a general-purpose procedure, which ideally should be written down and revised at regular intervals. It ensures that *dreams* can be made *real*. The "appreciation" methodology described later can be used for both the "big life-plan" and for solving more day-to-day decisions such as what car should you buy. First, the big plan.

Decide on your goals and write them down

Life planning is not just a straightforward "to-do" list or an inventory of shopping items or telephone calls to be made. Life planning starts out by you personally identifying your big ambitions – for how can you prioritise your day-to-day activities if your ultimate goal is not clear?

Philosophical generalities are inadmissible. "Be Happy" is not a goal – it may be an obvious prerequisite, but specifics are required. Write them down. Try to include 10 items. Try it now. For example, some goals might be:

- Climb Mount Everest / Snowdon / Eiffel Tower / that tree in the garden
- Cycle / sail / walk round the country / world / village
- Set up a business in a desirable activity
- Join the army
- Work in a dress shop
- Sell houses
- Buy junk and sell antiques
- Work in the City
- Become a writer / actor / politician / doctor / barrister / monk / pop star
- Get married to a rich bloke and have four kids.
- Live in a nice house with servants
- Live on a beach in a hot country
- Live on a huge estate with horses and ride every day.

Be bold. Be honest. Include even your most outrageous dreams, since if you do not alert yourself to them, you will never achieve them. Do not exclude goals because you think you cannot afford them or might not have the talent. Life is full of people who actually achieved what they wished for, simply out of sheer determination.

The reverse is more obvious: if you do not believe you can accomplish something, you almost certainly won't! If you start out imagining that you cannot do something, you will most likely fail. Self-belief is fundamental. If you lack assurance, remember you do not need any confidence simply to *write down* an ambition. So if you really, really want to do something, now is the time to include it in your 10 items. Yes, 10. Go on, do it now! This is your dream list.

If you are a couple, married or not, each of you should write your own list of 10 independently – and no peeking. By all means compare notes later, but the aim is to draw out what you personally really want to do. If you end up with a blank piece of paper, you are not trying hard enough. You are lucky to be alive on a mostly beautiful planet with an amazing abundance of exciting places to go to, things to do: so much to do – so little time. To have no ambition is a total waste of life and is a prescription for misery. Having a set of specific goals, planning them and then achieving them is just about the best way of ensuring happiness and life-long contentment that I can imagine.

Having perused your list, rewrite it in desirability order. Put the goals that excite you most at the top. You might even eliminate one or two as you write. Try to end up with at least three in your final choice. If, when you look at this final list you sigh because of a goal that is now missing, perhaps it should be reinserted. One trick is to imagine you only have 12 months to live. What would you *then* want to pick and in what order?

Now is also the time to eliminate the preposterous or the really unattainable. While I encouraged you to list even your most outrageous dreams, you will never become a pop idol if you cannot sing in tune – well let's at least say it's not impossible (I have heard some!) – but unlikely. Matching your ambitions with your personal ability is more likely to work out. So now strike out goals which might need a special talent that you know you just do not have. I wanted to learn to play the piano but I just did not have what it took and had to give up eventually. I was actually totally useless, playing with boring mathematical precision but little natural talent and feeling! I will not try again.

The next important step is to consider what you actually **do** day to day, how you fill your waking hours and just where your *big ambition* list fits in. Daily activities can be divided into three simple priorities:

A. "Must do" as a first priority (eg earn some money, pay the bills),
B. "Need to do" sometime, but only after the "Must do" items are done (eg ring up and say hello to mum and dad, decorate the house, service the car),
C. "Like to do" or "wants" – but when there is time and money (eg have a holiday, buy a better car / house / TV, write a book, travel etc).

Differentiating between "need" and "want" is an important concept. One "needs" food, clothing and shelter. You may "want" a bigger car or a better house. While "wants" are perfectly legitimate aims, they should be separated out and are secondary to one's basic needs. Moreover, as I said earlier, "wants" should match one's ability to achieve them. A blind person is unlikely to become a world class pistol shot. Be ambitious by all means, but a touch of realism is advantageous. Needs always come before Wants.

Now for the final and most important step. Your original list of 10 big ambitions, having now been distilled down to a few attainable ones, must be integrated into your A, B, C list of daily activities. It is now when the real action comes in. If your biggest ambition is, say, to climb Everest, an 'A' priority might be to buy a book about it *this afternoon*. A 'B' item might then be to join a mountaineering club. The actual plan to climb Everest is in the 'C' list. You will need to do a lot of A and B stuff first. But, most importantly, your ambition is now an official, listed aim and one you need to seriously plan for. It is on *The Plan* and it is looked at daily and is no longer just a dream.

Incidentally, one's goals need not always have a financial bias. Some people might choose living as a recluse and writing poetry as their number one goal. In which case their plan requires only very modest financial ambitions. But if you want to own a 50-acre estate, breeding racehorses, you have to earn a certain amount of money first. So you would have to think how you would do this – say, become a money dealer in the City: it may be highly stressful but you could earn loads of money. So by all means have a plan in separate stages.

Your own goals will be specific. Having decided on them, you can immediately prioritise your time – the highest priority gets the first available slot.

Make an "appreciation" to solve problems

The components of the plan needed to achieve your goal should be entered on your daily A, B, C activity list. One way of deciding on these components is to do what the army called an "appreciation" of the situation, which leads to successful planning and problem solving. The procedure is better when it is written out, as the key to it is dispassionate reasoning rather than simple intuition. The final plan should result from a pure intellectual assessment of the facts, rather than "fixing" the facts to support instinctive hunches or pre-sentiments.

Select one of your pre-listed goals at a time. Restate it as a simple *aim*: say "To climb Mount Everest". It should be a single statement and not a series of aims. There are then four basic steps.

Firstly, list all the *factors* affecting the achievement of that aim, without qualification.

Next, list each of the possible *courses open* for the necessary actions to achieve the aim, together with listed *advantages* and *disadvantages*.

Then, decide which of the above courses should, on the balance of the pros and cons, be the *course to be adopted*.

Finally, you then make your detailed *plan* of how to achieve the *aim* based on the *course adopted*. Keep the paper on which your deliberations were written for future reference in case you need to make a mid-course change.

Why write down the plan?

There is no doubt that committing actions to writing focuses the mind and weeds out woolly thinking. There is also a tendency sometimes for one to ignore the facts since you may already have a plan in your mind and "*nothing is going to change it*". There is also a tendency to make spontaneous judgements and select only those factors that support that initial instinct. It is essential to be very impartial and logical about a plan, almost ruthlessly determined, as this is your future and possibly your family's future, and you cannot afford to make mistakes.

The plan is the detail as to how each goal that you have now decided upon is to be achieved. The format can be as detailed as you like, but it should be integrated into your daily A, B C to-do list. This ensures it is seldom out of mind and really focuses the mind on the job in hand.

I use a little hand-held computer which includes a "task list". The advantage for me is that it already has a mechanism for recording three priorities, using High, Normal and Low: this is directly analogous to A, B and C. Also, it can be constantly updated with ease.

Those who do not like computers enough to include them in one's life planning processes (shame), might be content with a simple "day book" divided into three sections – you've guessed already – A, B and C. Or have three books. The relevant written item in the list is then simply crossed out when it is achieved.

Spin or fact and a political planning failure?

As an aside, there is a classic example of where an intuitive plan was made without proper, rigorous analysis and which then needed a false appreciation to be contrived later in order to justify it. It was the plan to invade Iraq in 2003. Bush simply wanted to go – partly to finish off what his father failed to do, and partly to ensure one of America's "gas stations" was kept online. Blair needed to follow Bush, partly because he believed we need America as our "best friend" to help our defence, and partly because he thought a good war improved his chance of another term in office, as Thatcher once did with the Falklands. (You may think differently.)

But, as we now know, the "appreciation" actually put to the people by the government – the infamous dossier – proved to be badly flawed. It was a triumph for the emotional appeal rather than a clear analysis of hard-nosed facts. It was simple spin. The stated reasons for the war were actually quite false – finding weapons of mass destruction. When that reason proved baseless they changed the game by claiming "we got Saddam out, didn't we?" Let this world-class debacle be a lesson to all those who might be tempted to tweak their own life "appreciations". Be totally honest, objective and dispassionate if you want to ensure you arrive at a truly optimal solution.

Why is budgeting important

Charles Dickens wrote about a certain Wilkins Micawber in his *David Copperfield* for whom something was always going to "come up". His advice was simple:

> "Annual income twenty pounds, annual expenditure nineteen nineteen and six, result happiness. Annual income twenty pounds, annual expenditure twenty pounds ought and six, result misery."

In more modern currency: income £20 and expenditure £19.99p – result happiness. Income £20 and expenditure £20.01p – result misery. So happiness cost nothing more than 2p.

Dee has always said (and she was once a marriage guidance counsellor) that *budgeting* is one secret of a happy marriage. Couples can so easily fall out if they have money worries. Simply planning for expenditure to always fall below income is a major step forward. So make a personal budget. Get a bank account. Read the later section in this book on *Finance*.

A budget consists of a detailed list of all your recurring expenditure items, including tax. Include in this list your net regular income as well as any possible speculative income as a separate item. Your planned expenditure should be less than your regular, secure monthly net income. If not, you have to reduce or eliminate one or more selected cost area – *wants,* like smoking, or holidays rather than *needs* like rent or utility bills.

Expenditure items should ideally also include a set amount to save for holidays and, if possible, a retirement pension and also a reserve for unforeseen contingencies. Update it regularly. Actually it is easy to do, and quite fun when you see it all work out in practice. I remember the great sense of joy whenever we discovered a small surplus over our budget. The only difficult bit is getting round to doing it. How about tonight?

So remember the Micawber principle: happiness is a positive cash flow!

Expenditure planning is more important to plan than income. You might like to keep a book or a spreadsheet and enter what you have *actually* spent over say a monthly period – it might surprise you! A business runs on cash flow planning and a record of planned against actual expenditure is vital so that reasons for any variances can be investigated. Similarly a household account covering basic expenditure is very valuable. Basic items include rates, utilities, food, mortgage, transport and fuel, tax, insurance, savings, pension, household maintenance, and so on. Other "luxury" expenditure (eg holidays) would be paid from a budget surplus – if any.

Another excellent idea (Dee thought of it, naturally) is to pay as many regular bills as you can by standing order or direct debit. It immediately takes the worry and work out of writing out regular cheques, finding envelopes and stamps and posting them off – usually late and incurring extra charges. Direct debits are the best: they are free, simple and safe, since if any debtor takes an incorrect amount you can legally demand it is repaid to you by your bank without question. Standing orders are only for fixed amounts. You can pay practically anything this way today. Internet banking is also wonderfully convenient.

When you are on holiday or away from home it is comforting to think that all the bills are being paid automatically without any effort by you. That is always assuming you have budgeted correctly and funds are in place beforehand. A small overdraft facility to allow for larger and less frequent bills to be settled is worthwhile if you have insufficient cash to start with.

Dee has a good idea for those paid weekly. Take your money out a day later each week: in other words, make it last eight days. After seven weeks, you have gained a whole week's pay – free. Magic!

In short, worries about money are insidious. But with careful planning and budgeting, which itself can be pleasurable, your life really is less stressful and more fulfilling.

Summary

One might say that the purpose of life is life with a purpose. To make a plan and then to achieve its objectives is an immensely satisfying experience. Moreover, a plan that ensures a positive cash flow is a definite prerequisite.

I would also say that these last couple of sections are perhaps the most crucial in the book. If you disagree, I suggest you reread them and actually try writing down your wish lists as suggested.

Education

I can encapsulate this section thus: the more you know, the richer your life becomes in every respect. The more able you are to think logically, the easier it is to solve problems and move through life more effortlessly. The better your education, the wider is your scope for discovering pleasurable pursuits. If you think education is a waste of time, try ignorance, for it is all around you. Ignorance causes infinitely more problems and unhappiness than learning.

At any educational establishment, it is essential to be curious and interested. Some may think it is being *big* to be nonchalant and *grown up* to show disregard for teaching and teachers. It is the biggest mistake of their lives. Young minds learn quickly: take full advantage of this unique opportunity to train your mind and learn something about the world – it is immensely satisfying.

Good private schools (not all of them by any means) offer better opportunities for educating youngsters than most state schools, although many local schools can produce excellent results. This is partly because private schools can often afford better facilities and more motivated teachers. However, more importantly, their pupils come from fee-paying families who are all clearly *committed* to education, so the atmosphere is bound to be somewhat more positive. Private education is very expensive but at least it can be exclusive in the best sense. That is not to say those who cannot afford private education are not committed – some are, some not.

It must be difficult for a pupil who is anxious to learn but finds himself in a disruptive, difficult state school where education seems to be a second priority because a handful of pupils come from a troublesome background. Like terrorism, it only needs a few extremists to make life hell for the moderates. Many good teachers avoid such unruly classes if they can, unless they are unusually dedicated. Successful learning is often more to do with who is within the classroom rather than who is in front of it. Willing fellow pupils can make a world of difference.

It is difficult for the majority of parents who do rate education but cannot afford to go private. They have more difficult choices as they may have to move house in order to live in a better catchment area.

The private/state school option has nothing to do with snobbery, but politicians often make education a class issue because only the rich can afford private education. Actually, only the rich can afford anything expensive! It must surely be far better to encourage wealth than despise it: it is far better to encourage centres of excellence than to dismantle them. That only happens in ill-informed third-world countries, doesn't it? Of course, state education should be improved, but not at the expense of the private sector. If you cannot afford private education (and sadly few can) at least one might be able to move to an area with good schools.

Teaching and learning are very different

Teaching skills are unfortunately very variable. When I was young, I learnt most from the enthusiasts, those who could make their subject interesting enough to leave their students craving more. I believe teachers should focus primarily on the more exciting uses of their subject, rather than prattle on about the dreariest aspects. What is the use of learning algebra unless you can see an interesting application? Pose an interesting problem first, and *then* show its power. Take the pupils out on a fact-finding mission. Ask them how aeroplanes stay up, why satellites do not fall to earth. How do car engines work? Put to them questions, such as how do we know how far away the stars are, how hot are they, and what they are made of? These examples are male biased I know – these were things which fascinated me – but I make a plea to would-be teachers to focus on *why* we need to know things, and not just how to pass boring exams.

My history teacher was a blathering bore and, as a result, I took no interest in the subject then, and much regretted it later. A temporary teacher did take over for a week, and he told us some fascinating historical stories that really brought the subject alive for a fleeting moment, sadly soon to fade when Blunder Bore returned. What *do* they teach them at teacher training college?

Match ambition to skills

Not everyone can become a brain surgeon. Not everyone can become a skilled carpenter. There is currently a political trend to expect everyone to be able to go to university. This can cause much unhappiness when students find themselves unable to cope with an academic routine: you cannot force a square peg into a round hole without causing damage. Matching ability to ambition is more important than ambition at any price. There are plenty of non-academic skills in great demand, and these can be immensely satisfying and desirable.

University

If you have the talent and the desire, three years at university is a really worthwhile experience. It is not so much about the subject itself but more about learning how to think, how to argue logically and how to express complex ideas in a simple way, and on paper. The subject is clearly important if you have a profession in mind, such as medicine or law. If not, pick a subject you enjoy and are good at: it need not be career related – deciding on that can wait.

One also learns about self-discipline at university – a very important personal attribute. I remember being very surprised to learn that university lectures were not compulsory, unlike school lessons. I found this sudden introduction to freedom of choice rather unsettling at first and, frankly, I initially abused it. But just as suddenly maturity arrives when you realise you are your own master, and no longer an instructed child. If you choose to skip lectures for some short-term gratification (like a lie-in), *you* are the ultimate loser – no one else.

In my experience, not that many students actually end up in jobs directly connected with their degree. I read Engineering and ended up in Finance. Our son, Robert, studied Marine Biology but his career took him into Information Technology and Finance. While it helps to know what your future career might be before choosing your degree course, it is not essential. Neither is it essential to know your future at school either. It is a shame that parents often cajole their offspring into deciding what they want to do far too early. The longer you wait, the more information you can gather about your talents and desires, and therefore the more suitable and satisfying will be your eventual choice.

Summary

Get the best education you can. Take full advantage of it. Don't waste chances. It will make all the difference to your life in every respect. Don't be in too much of a hurry to decide your adult role. Gather information about yourself first. Choose something you love doing and in which you know you have the required skills and competence. Non-academic skills are in great demand.

Match ambition with ability. Earning more money does not necessarily mean you are more successful. Achieving success in whatever you choose leads to genuine contentment – this is the real secret.

Are you an entrepreneur?

What follows is an extract of a talk I gave to some young students in Portsmouth in 1997 when I was chairman of software company, Dunstan Thomas Limited. It is reproduced here in simple bullet point format for those who would like to try their hand in business.

Being an entrepreneur and running your own business can not only provide you with a good living but can also be a very satisfying activity. Setting out any aim, and then actually achieving it, however modest that aim, gives one a terrific lift – close to ecstasy. Running a business is just like that. Experiencing the hum of humans engaged in profitable commercial activity, particularly when it is all devised and headed by you, is pure euphoria. However, not everyone can make a success out of being an entrepreneur if they lack some key attributes.

Any business has to be run primarily to make a profit. If it does not make a profit, it clearly makes a loss and so, eventually, it will die. If it makes a profit, it will grow and provide more security, more employment and more profits – and more tax for the country to share. A successful business means a profitable business, not just one with a large turnover.

Having the right personal characteristics to be a successful business person is like listing the ingredients of a tasty cake: all the ingredients need to be present in the right proportions to get a good result. Sometimes, if one individual has a few missing ingredi-ents, collaborating with someone else who can make up for them can be helpful.

This is a summary of some of the essential personal ingredients for success:

Drive – an attitude of mind

- Determination – the key motivator
- Persistence – stick at it, regardless of hurdles
- Enthusiasm – be excited
- Positiveness – you know you will succeed
- Risk taking – accept that risk is necessary to achieve rewards
- Energy – be prepared for hard work and long hours

Character – sound and straight

- Common sense – a basic prerequisite
- Honesty – being trustworthy
- Good judgement – making good decisions
- Integrity – being reliable and eventually respected
- Consistency – don't change your mind too often
- Open-mindedness – listen to others

Academic skills

- Literacy– ability to express well on paper
- Numeracy – ability to create and understand a business plan

Useful abilities

- Creativity
- Computer literacy
- Languages (if trading abroad)
- Bookkeeping or accountancy skills
- Salesmanship
- Relevant technical knowledge

Capital

- Ask dad or other supporters for the loan of seed capital (possibly 30% of the total required) and use a high street bank loan for the balance (70%)

If you reckon you have most of the right ingredients and love the idea of running your own business, the first action is to pick a business involving something you enjoy and feel you would be good at doing. Then:

Initial actions

- Discuss your ideas with a successful friend
- Research your market
- Analyse and compare the competition
- Identify a niche
- Draft a conservative business plan

- Talk to an experienced accountant
- Talk to a friendly banker
- Organise finance
- Redraft the business plan if necessary
- Organise communications (fax, telephone, e-mail etc)
- Draft sales literature, notepaper, business cards
- Launch!

Other points

- Start slowly, constantly analysing progress
- *Promise* less to clients, customers and associates but *achieve* more
- Draw the absolute minimum amount of personal cash early on
- Aim to repay short-term debts before you reward yourself
- Control costs ruthlessly
- Run a cash book and review it weekly
- Insist on monthly management accounts showing actual income and expenditure compared to planned, and explain the variances
- Good ideas are easy to come by – making them profitable is tougher
- Work hard and long in the initial months
- Listen particularly to the advice of *successful* business people
- Exploit emerging technology

Even with all these ingredients, life is seldom predictable. Setbacks will occur but, with good planning and a cool head, they can be beaten. Similarly, opportunities will turn up and sound judgement and good advice will enable you to exploit them.

Finally, remember a business **has** to be a success – it **has** to make money – otherwise it will eventually fail – and worse still end up as a big personal liability. So take it very seriously but enjoy it as well. If it is not fun – do not do it.

One further point: it is worth stressing the importance of forming a good relationship with a bank. Cash is the lifeblood of any business, and cash flow and its management is vital. Banks *like* lending money – that is where *their* profit comes from. However, they only lend to people likely to pay it back!

The easiest way to get on good terms with your bank is always to do what you say you will do – or do better. If you say to a lender that they will be repaid inside a month – mean it. Never over-promise, thinking that it might impress. Under achieving will certainly *d*epress! Banks prefer conservative estimates. Banks also understand plan changes, as long as they know in advance. Nothing is worse than an unauthorised overdraft: it is not only bad manners, but it signals to the bank that you are disorganised at best, or in trouble at worse.

Manage your bank relationships well, demonstrate conspicuous integrity, and they will then look after you when you need them most.

Summary

If you want to be the boss – promote yourself – set up your own business. First check out if you have what it takes – not everyone has, and failure in business can be painful. Be sure you really want to take the risks and work that hard. Research your market, talk to **successful** people about your ideas (better not listen to those who have never been their own successful boss). Read books about business in general and your chosen business in particular. Subscribe to relevant magazines. Join relevant societies and clubs. Get stuck in.

Then make a conservative plan for at least the next two years, indicating monthly income, all expenditure, broken down to its components, and the resultant cumulative cash flow. A new business will usually start out with a negative cash flow, but eventually it must turn the corner and replace the borrowed money. Allow for interest. Use a spreadsheet by preference. Under promise but over achieve. Read the next section about running a business.

Discuss the plan with your chosen accountant; arrange the finance and then **launch** with a blaze of publicity. **Good Luck!**

Running a business

Dee and I have set up and run a number of successful business enterprises over the years, one employing over 600 staff. As a result, we have formed some useful opinions about what works and what doesn't, some of which I have summarised below. Much is applied common sense, but it is important to actually adopt these principles rather than just read and talk about them. That is not to say do *not* read: on the contrary, read every possible management book you can find, but form a personal consensus and then act on it. I am now more able to detect the difference between a successful winner and a potential failure by his or her basic attitude to business.

- Consider carefully all the points discussed in the previous section and decide whether you are the right type of person to be an entrepreneur before wasting your time.
- Research your proposed market thoroughly and then plan meticulously, particularly cash flow. Identify critical elements of the business plan, and give them special attention and future focus.
- Choose you support team not by picking bored friends at a loose end, but select the best people you can find. Recruit more on *attitude* than on paper qualifications. A committed employee can always learn new skills: over-qualified but under-motivated people can soon become unhappy passengers.
- Be candid with new staff. Do not over promise or overpay. Be clear what you expect of them. Write down their precise role and their performance targets. Measure their performance regularly against the targets you have set.

- Put round pegs in round holes – do not expect exceptional performance from untrained, unsuitable or uninformed staff. Provide the best training. If you think training is expensive, try ignorance!
- Care for all members of staff whatever their role. "Who cares wins". Ruthlessness is not a winner's attribute.
- Staff pay comes before anything, so always reserve for it. They are not the risk taker, you are. In return for honouring all the commitments you make to your staff, you will eventually attract loyalty and ultimately respect.
- Ensure your customers enjoy the best possible level of service.
- Strive for excellence: constantly improve all procedures. Let you staff and customers know your mission statement.
- Analyse income and expenditure at least monthly: identify variances against plan and correct detected problems immediately.
- Constantly observe the market you are in and your competitors. Compare performances. Identify niches. Large companies need to dominate the standard commodity market and so leave niches to the smaller firms. Take advantage of being small.
- Good marketing is essential. Strive for free editorial comment rather than pay for adverts. If advertising is essential, national advertising usually beats local advertising for overall effect unless your market is local only.
- Exploit good opportunities when they arise: it could be a takeover or a new market for which you have appropriate skills, but always investigate.
- Perform a regular SWOT analysis: identify you firm's core competences and Strengths, then their Weaknesses: look at all Opportunities and identify Threats. Be open-minded.
- Always act fairly and honestly. Mistakes are inevitable: compensate disgruntled customers with an open admission and they will soon become supporters.
- Prepare careful agendas for regular operational meetings. Meetings are necessary to decide on specific actions and responsibilities, not just to talk.
- Remember the four principles of management: Plan, Organise, Motivate and Control. Insist middle management operate on these principles too.

This is not an exhaustive list, but a mind dump of those items that Dee and I have identified as being important in over 50 years of working experience including, in my case, 12 very useful years in the army. Sandhurst trains cadets to become leaders – assuming the right basic qualities are there at the outset.

In a war, there can be massive confusion and on-going life and death situations, all in appalling conditions: leadership is essential to get oneself and one's comrades through this fog of war. Business is not quite so fraught and financial matters are seldom relevant on the battlefield where "loss" would have a more tragic meaning. However, in most other management activities there are similarities. As with the military system, *leadership* is probably the one word I would use to summarise the ultimate quality needed for business success as well.

Investments, finance and mortgages

This is my specialist subject, having been involved with financial services since 1970. Therefore, I have lots to be opinionated about! I have written another book, freely available online at www.mortgagesExposed.com, which is mostly about the mechanics of mortgage and loan products. Some may find it a bit heavy going, but I have extracted some of the more constructive bits for this book. My aim is to present some general principles, which should last a long time, rather than make specific recommendations that may be fashionable. You may need to read this section several times for the pennies to drop. (Is that a pun?)

First of all, let me run through some useful generalities about investments, many of which apply to business as well. Personal financial planning strategy can be split into three periods: Youth, middle age and retirement.

In the early days of adulthood, most of us have to struggle to earn enough to pay the bills, let alone start a pension plan. For such youngsters, trying to save for the long term is rarely possible as there are too many short-term demands on income. Setting up a life with a partner is a particularly expensive activity: just building the nest takes up a lot of cash! Budgeting for day-to-day living is the priority here, so short-term deposits or a flexible mortgage account (see later) are more relevant. Now is a good time to enjoy yourself, when you are fit and fearless, so don't weigh yourself down with heavy savings plans at this stage. However, as soon as some surplus income arises, you are into the second period.

This second period usually occurs when you have developed a more established career and can afford to put something away. The objective now is to build surplus capital while you are earning so you can later convert it back into income when you retire. This is a *capital growth* strategy period.

The final period is when you cease having to work for reward. That period, in financial terms, is when you have amassed sufficient capital to be able to *afford* retirement. Do not rely on the state pension alone – it is nowhere near sufficient! At this point in your life, the capital you have built up must then be turned back into a lifetime income, which is as safe, reliable and as inflation resistant as possible and tax efficient as well. This is the final *income* strategy period.

Investment types fall into four main categories:

1. *Fixed capital*, such as bank or building society deposits. The initial capital invested remains constant – there is no capital growth. Interest is payable, which usually fluctuates in line with market rates. Interest can be reinvested as new capital and added to the original capital.
2. *Fixed Interest*, such as government stock, or gilts. The *interest* is fixed throughout a given term but the capital value fluctuates in line with the market's perception of the value of the fixed income. For dated stock the capital is always returned at maturity at par. Falling market rates for interest (eg bank base rates) will increase the value and vice versa. It is more a professionals market.
3. *Real assets*, such as ordinary shares (equities) or investment property, which can produce an increasing income (dividend) which is broadly linked to inflationary pressures. Capital values can still fluctuate with market sentiment and confidence and individual shares can crash to nothing, but the long-term trend is to beat inflation.
4. *Fashionable assets*, such as antiques, wines, fine art, precious stones and metals. These assets produce no income to facilitate valuing their worth and are thus subject to pure supply and demand: the demand relates to the current fashion. Gold is slightly different as it traditionally rises in value when there is world economic uncertainty – and vice versa.

Supply and demand is the foremost economic principle of a free market. In simple terms, the price of any particular widely available item is a balance between the demand for it and the supply of it. The higher the demand (because of the attractiveness of the product and the number of people desiring it) the higher the price is pushed: conversely, if the product is in plentiful supply and easy to obtain, prices are forced down.

Supply and demand interact with each other until an equilibrium price is reached – the market price. This principle applies equally to investment products. The concept is not perfect, and is actually more complex than the simple definition above, but it is perfectly valid for a free market and a democracy like ours. Businesses rely on supply and demand, and competitive pressures usually ensure the consumer ends up the winner.

For any type of investment, there are three ultimate investment goals that most people would aspire to:

1. *Safety*. You want the investment to be as safe as the Bank of England. Words like "guarantee" feature highly. Losing capital is not an option.
2. *Performance*. You want it to grow spectacularly by at least 20% a year, preferably 100% per annum, or provide an income at the same level. Oh, and tax free as well!
3. *Flexibility*. You need to be able to cash it in without penalty at a minute's notice – or even sooner.

However, you just cannot have *everything* you want and you certainly cannot achieve all three of these aims at once, so compromise is inevitable.

For example, a building society deposit (fixed capital) scores highly under *security* – no one has ever lost a bean in the last hundred years or more from a building society deposit and there is even a government-sponsored guarantee for 90% of your investment up to a maximum figure as well.

However, you certainly will not get a return of 20% per annum. You would be lucky to get a return of just under bank rate and then there is income tax to pay. 3% to 4% pa net might have been just possible in mid 2004 when base rates were around 4.75%. Whenever the word "guaranteed" appears in investment literature, the performance will always be at the "low" end of the scale. If you are ever offered a guaranteed investment with a performance figure that seems too good to be true, it almost certainly is!

Nevertheless, you would be able to cash in most deposit accounts very quickly, so such deposits are flexible as separate investments. When measuring up a deposit-type investment with our three aims, aims one

(*Safety*) and three (*Flexibility*) score high but aim two (*Performance*) scores badly.

Conversely, investing in stocks and shares can provide very high potential *Performance* but not much in the *Safety* department. Over a long period (over 10 years), an average portfolio of shares has, in general, not only beaten inflation, but by a good margin. However, as they say in the advertisements, share prices can, and do, go down as well as up and the past is not necessarily a guide to the future. But you can cash-in a share almost immediately, so excellent *Flexibility* too.

Property in general, including commercial property such as offices, shops, and warehouses, has also proved to be a good investment in the long term and is probably safer than stocks and shares, and certainly less turbulent.

However, you cannot cash-in a building as quickly as a share. You cannot cash-in a *part* of a building either, which you can with a share portfolio. Consequently, property scores low on *Flexibility* but it is not so bad on *Performance* and less risky than shares in general.

Therefore, in summary, choosing an investment requires a compromise between *Safety*, *Performance* and *Flexibility*. Returns can be improved by sacrificing flexibility. Stunning returns can only be achieved by taking significant risk. Not everyone can stomach too much risk so. for them, rewards are going to be nominal only, such as with building societies.

Let me reiterate my earlier warning. There is no investment that provides higher-than-average performance without higher-than-average risk, given the same level of flexibility. Despite this, investors are continuously duped into parting with their cash for risky ventures that are marketed as being more safe than they really are – and some are downright fraudulent. A fool and his money are soon parted, so be vigilant.

Always apply the risk–reward measure. If you want the rewards – be prepared for the risks. Always look behind promised numbers. Be suspicious of anything out of the ordinary. Particularly, avoid start-up companies looking for venture capital unless you have money to burn. If you want to make a small fortune – invest a large fortune in a start-up. Most fail.

Most long-term collective investments such as pensions, unit trusts or insurance bonds go in for conventional real assets such as ordinary shares (equities) or property. This is because the returns are likely to beat inflation as a minimum over the longer term. Equities pay regular dividends that usually rise as the business improves and expands. This increasing dividend income stream improves the share price, which is ultimately set by supply and demand. A rising income obviously costs more than a fixed income, so the initial yield for equities is usually lower than for a fixed-capital or fixed-income investment.

Choosing a specific listed share is not an easy process. Not only must the chosen business and its employees succeed with a viable business plan, but also the management must be competent enough to deliver the numbers,and then the market place must value the asset correctly. You will most likely never have met these people, nor seen either their office or factory. These key aspects are difficult for the lay investor to judge,as the information made available is not always comprehensive enough. If the business fails and the shares become worthless, you could lose your entire investment. But that is never so with a direct property investment, which is at least always worth something, even if it is just a warehouse.

In my view, individual, listed shares are best avoided for all the above reasons. However, a well-managed unit trust is a different proposition since it consists of a professionally-chosen portfolio of at least 20 different shares which is designed to focus on specific *sectors*, which can be more or less risky –you choose. The income from a unit trust (which can be reinvested for growth) usually rises every year despite any wild fluctuations in the capital value. This is because the fund invests in a spread of shares: the larger the spread the lower the risk, but the less the potential gain or the nearer to "average" it will be.

One such sector is called a "tracker", which aims just to match a defined stock market index. This is no mean achievement historically, and in the long term will probably produce an acceptable performance with minimal risk as shares *en mass* are less likely to fail suddenly. You may miss some lucky upside opportunities: but I would far rather be happy with an expected, albeit average, performance than be miserable with a possible negative one that *could* have been terrific.

How to pick shares is a big subject and quite beyond the scope of this book. Independent advice is always needed before you invest: sadly, the quality of such advice is seldom high, and rarely independent. There are a few fee-charging advisers who are unbiased and will offset commissions earned against their fee but they are hard to find. Most advisers will recommend you spread your investments. The mix would be based on risk and flexibility – some capital in deposits, some in low risk some in high risk, the latter being money you can afford to lose.

Buying individual shares and unit trusts is a question of good timing as the markets fluctuate daily, usually unpredictably. The best adage I know is "buy in gloom and sell in boom". In other words, buy when it is easy to buy (when no one wants to invest, only sell) and sell when everyone else is buying (as long as the selling price is higher than the buying price of course). While there are other adages, I suggest you work it out for yourself rather than rely on the alleged pundits who usually have a different agenda from the actual punter. Remember that a stockbroker makes money whether he is buying or selling shares on your behalf, regardless of your profit.

I believe a pension and an ISA to be worth having, provided it invests in tracker funds, unless you are personally au fait with the investment scene. Both are uniquely tax-privileged funds. ISAs are more flexible but not as tax efficient. Take advice from more than one source before committing. Avoid bank- or insurance-managed funds, as their performance is usually lacklustre since investment management it is not their principle activity. Independent groups are usually better choices to manage your investments provided that *investment management* is their sole activity.

A SIPP (Self Invested Pension Plan) is ideal for the knowledgeable investor, and is a particularly useful vehicle for investing long term in commercial property, as both rental income and capital growth is entirely tax free.

Purchasing your home

In the past, one of the finest investment of all time was to buy your own house. You live in it rent-free, the growth is tax-free and you can borrow practically every penny to buy it, at interest rates that, in the past, have been less than the growth rate of the property itself – so you even profit by borrowing rather than paying cash.

While house prices can, and do, go down as well as up, the long-term trend is to rise at the same rate as average earnings. This has certainly worked in my lifetime and I see no reason why it should not continue to work long term in the future, despite more short-term variations now than in the past.

Renting a house is fine during the period when you have neither yet developed a reliable income, nor built up a modest deposit, let alone saved up for furniture. Renting is usually more economic than buying only if you plan to move within around two years, simply because the cost of buying and selling a house would probably outweigh any capital growth over such a short period by more than the rent otherwise paid. Nevertheless, I recommend you buy a house as soon as possible using the largest, longest, cheapest mortgage you can find. Even if you let the house and use the rental income to enable you to rent another house to live in, you are very likely to profit from the purchase in the long run.

Renting usually requires no more than a month's rent as deposit, a regular rental payment in advance and, depending on the tenancy terms, the property owner usually looks after major repairs. Renting a home is straightforward, quick and easy and can be for short or long term. However, the money expended on rent is gone forever. Rent always rises with inflation over the medium to long term. On the other hand, mortgage payments fluctuate about a level norm depending only on interest rates. The money expended on a mortgage over the long term is usually far less than the capital growth of the property. In the long term, a property bought with a mortgage still seems to be an outstanding investment.

Many years go I remember a colleague saying to me "Buy land – they don't make it anymore, but they do make more people. A constant supply and increasing demand means only one thing – prices go up!" Manhattan Island in America was bought for a total of just $24 in 1626 – we now know it as New York and parts of it are probably worth over $24 per square millimetre today!

Investing in property

Buying property for investment purposes has always proved a wise choice for many people provided some basic rules are followed. If this interests you, please read more in www.mortgagesExposed.com. However, let me summarise some of the principles.

There are two broad categories of property investments – *residential* (often called buy-to-let) and *commercial* (offices, shops warehouses, factories etc). The former are relatively simple to purchase, require more management and can give a good return but with some risk. Commercials can provide less risk and less management but need more initial capital and more care in selecting.

It is almost always better to purchase property with a mortgage, preferably interest-only. This is called *gearing* and is a crucial concept to grasp.

An easy example of gearing for buy-to-let properties

Say you had £10,000 to invest. You buy a £100,000 house using a £90,000 mortgage, so your initial £10,000 is the deposit. Ignore fees and costs for the moment.

Assume the house is then let to a tenant, and the rental income just covers the interest-only mortgage payments. The monthly ownership cost is therefore zero – again forget maintenance costs for a moment.

Now let us say the house is sold for £105,000 a year later, which represented a 5% per annum property growth rate. After repaying the £90,000 interest-only mortgage, you are now left with £15,000. Your profit is £5,000, which is the amount remaining over after the sale less your original capital investment of £10,000.

In this simplified example, you have invested £10,000 and after one year received £15,000 – a profit of 50%. However, the underlying asset itself, the house, only appreciated by 5%. You have achieved an actual return on capital of 10 times the underlying asset growth! The *Internal Rate of Return* of your investment is 50% pa. Had you bought the house for cash with no mortgage, the return would have been only 5% pa and you would have needed 10 times as much capital. This remarkable result arises as a direct consequence of *gearing*. You have geared up by a multiple of 10 to increase a return of 5% to 50%, simply by borrowing. But there's more.

We first assumed there was no *net* income since the rent equalled the mortgage interest. However, say the property was actually rented out for £7,000 pa (about £135 per week) – that is a modest property yield of 7% pa and is possible in many areas of the UK.

If the £90,000 mortgage interest rate was say 6% pa, the interest payable in the year would come to £5,400 pa. Income £7,000, expenditure £5,400: the result is a net income of £1,600 per annum, ignoring expenses.

An income of £1,600 pa on an initial investment of £10,000 means a running income yield of 16% pa – from an investment yielding only 7%. So, not only have you achieved a capital growth of 50% but there is also an income of 16% pa as well – a total return of 66% in total in year one! Gearing enhances income as well as capital growth.

Is this really true? Surely it is not that easy? What are the snags? Well, first of all, reality always involves some friction, and tax, fees, costs and expenses will inevitably bring down the return. Nonetheless, the results from gearing can still be impressive and certainly exceed the basic return. The website mentioned earlier includes some useful spreadsheets and online tools to calculate the return after expenses. It is surprisingly good.

As I mentioned at the start, gearing is not without a certain amount of risk. The three main risks are:

1. The tenant might leave, or fail to pay, so producing a *void*. The mortgage would still need paying, so instead of receiving a positive monthly income, you find you are then paying *out* mortgage interest in full with no rent to help, so resulting in a *negative* income.
2. Mortgage interest rates could rise so that your initial margin between the rent coming in and the mortgage payment going out falls, or even becomes negative.
3. The property may fall in value. If it falls by more than the mortgage debt, you would *owe* money if you sold, and you would have what is called *negative equity*.

How can you minimise these very real risks?

1. Reduce the overall impact of voids by creating a *portfolio* of at least 10 buy-to-let investment properties, preferably in different areas. It is unlikely for all of them to go into a void situation at the same time, thus minimising the chance of negative income overall. The more properties you own and the greater the spread of risk, the safer the overall investment.
2. Put some rent aside as a reserve for voids and maintenance.
3. Fix your interest rate and/or borrow less money. The overall return may then fall, but so will the risk. It is possible to purchase a "swap" or a "cap" to prevent the mortgage interest rate applying to *any* loan of the same amount increasing beyond pre-set limits for pre-set periods. Banks have details of various instruments of this type.

4. Choose your property well and research the area carefully: this skill improves with experience. With buy-to-let, smaller, cheaper properties, usually produce the best income yields, but not always the best capital growth. On the other hand, larger, grander residences might grow more, but the income yield is less attractive. Choose property to match the rental market, not your own personal taste. Measure the return using tools such as those freely available from *www.mortgagesExposed.com*.

If the net income level is satisfactory, there is no real need to sell an investment property in time of gloom. Even if the capital value falls, the rental income may well continue. Rents gradually rise over the years, increasing your income and reducing the capital risk as your equity rises. An early sale would also give rise to capital gains tax. Only sell up if, after tax and charges, an opportunity for a better return arises elsewhere. Be prepared to invest further funds on repairs, maintenance and improvements. The mortgage loan can always be increased when the property has increased in value, and the extra used to finance portfolio expansion. But beware increasing it to a level beyond the net equity after capital gains tax.

If you choose *commercial* property, you can be very selective with your tenant who could even be a government body or at least a large public company unlikely to default on their rent. Moreover, commercial tenancies are for longer terms – typically 10 or more years, and the tenant pays for repairs and insurance. Such investments are less of a worry, but they tend to require larger investments. There are a few companies specialising in syndication so you can be a small spoke in a bigger wheel.

There are numerous subsections under the general term "commercial property". It is too big a subject for this book, but careful research pays dividends. However, geared commercial property investment can produce an above average return with risks that can be controlled – certainly with a lower risk than with direct investment in equities.

My personal taste is for modern commercial properties let to blue chip companies who are less likely to fail and for terms exceeding 10 years. At my age, I am in the investment *income* stage, so net yields are more important to me than capital growth. While the yields are slightly less for higher quality tenants, the mortgage rates that lenders charge are lower too: in these cases, the tenant is far more important than the landlord as far as a lender is concerned, and a 75% loan-to-value ratio can provide a very satisfactory level of gearing, with suitable interest rate hedges in place.

There may be times when property yields are lower than mortgage interest rates and a decent net income is not possible. Unless there are prospects for good capital growth, these properties are best avoided until markets rebalance. My own view is that a good property deal must provide either an early cash profit or an above average income.

Flexible mortgages

Going back to buying your own home, I thoroughly commend the use of a *flexible mortgage*, sometimes called an *offset* mortgage or a *current account mortgage*. In essence, you secure a loan of the very maximum your income and the property can provide, even if you only need a *proportion* of that loan to actually buy the house: the undrawn portion then becomes a *reserve*. You only pay interest on the amount actually outstanding day by day, and not the total possible loan.

You can draw on this reserve at any time and for almost any purpose during the term of the loan, in whole or in part, and for as short a time or as long as you wish. The interest rates charged are the same as a normal mortgage. The loan is a *secured* long-term mortgage – the safest type from any lender's perception. Mortgage lenders operate in a huge market where competition and market forces have pushed margins down to very fine levels, so the interest rate is usually the lowest possible.

You can also "invest" by paying money back into the mortgage account, even for a few days. Interest is calculated daily. Any credit instantly lowers the total debt and so reduces the interest you pay. You should therefore arrange all your income to be directed into your flexible mortgage account: your pay, dividends, sundry cheques and so on. Similarly, pay all your bills from the same account. Your overall loan falls the very day you make the credit: a lower loan, albeit temporary, immediately reduces the interest you pay on that portion.

Effectively, your "deposit" is earning interest at the gross mortgage rate. If you are borrowing at say 5.5% interest, your deposits will also earn 5.5% interest. Not only that, but there is no tax to pay on the interest – there is nothing to put on your tax return as you have simply *reduced* your mortgage interest. A 40% taxpayer would be enjoying an effective gross return of over 9% pa with total flexibility! So now you can have debt and savings at the same time with no loss of interest.

This mortgage product is one of the better ones produced by the financial services industry (I helped invent it!). It may not suit everyone. It does need some proactive behaviour to exploit its features to the full. Operating the account over the internet is extremely effective. You can set up a number of sub-accounts with names such as "Salary", "Rents", "Tax", "Holiday", "House Extension" and so on. Surplus cash can be moved instantly between these sub-accounts as often as you want. There is no need for complex external accounts for different purposes. Interest is "offset" on these accounts with your overall mortgage loan and you cannot earn a better deposit rate. It is one account for all purposes.

Credit cards

A credit card is still very useful to have and certainly safer than carrying around wads of cash. It provides protection against dodgy sales, and you can use it to make purchases over the internet. Nevertheless, using it for a loan is the worst thing you can do, as the interest rate is so high: credit card loans are treated as an unsecured debt and rates of over 20% (true rate) are not unknown. So pay off your credit card in full every month, using your flexible mortgage account to do so. Exploit the month's free credit these cards usually provide.

Inheritance tax

The taxman is not content to tax your income, your expenditure (with VAT), your business and investment profits and your capital gains – he taxes it all again when you die. The rate is a penal 40% on gifted assets in excess of a threshold of around £300,000 per person, which increases slightly each year. It is called inheritance tax – I suppose because the government inherits so much of your money.

While this subject may be of little interest to my younger readers, once you have children it does become an issue. Fortunately, there are a number of methods to reduce much of it. Making a gift and surviving seven years is one way, but the donor cannot enjoy any benefit of the gift. For example, gifting your own home but still living in it rent free, or retaining the income of any income-producing asset is ineffective. Specialist advice is necessary once you feel you have enough to leave and wish to do so. However, let me point out some strategies.

If you spend everything before both you and your spouse die, no inheritance tax is payable. It is, after all, your own money – you made it, you can spend it. Only if you had inherited some of your wealth is there possibly an obligation to pass it on so the next generation for them to enjoy the benefits as you did. Spending your own wealth is a realistic option. Even your own home can be "spent" by using one of the various home income schemes or home reversion schemes where you can extract capital from your house, but still be able to live in it until death.

Capital can also be used to purchase an *annuity*. This produces a guaranteed lifetime income until you (and your partner if a joint annuity) have died. Since the capital normally becomes valueless on death, there is no inheritance tax to pay. On the other hand, annuity income is higher than the interest you would otherwise achieve elsewhere since annuity income is augmented by a capital element. This is your originally invested capital spread over your theoretical life expectancy, or joint expectancy (last to die) for couples. Moreover, this capital element is tax-free.

The issuing insurance company guarantees your income for life regardless of when the last annuitant actually dies. They can take on the life expectancy risk since they deal with large numbers of people, so longevity for them becomes a mathematical average. They may lose out with those living for longer than average, but gain on the earlier-than-average deaths. It balances out for them. But you are personally insulated from the risk of running out of capital by their guarantee.

Annuities became unfashionable at the turn of the century due to falling interest rates and increasing life expectancy, but the principle advantages remain – income is enhanced with a capital element, and is guaranteed for life. There are many different varieties of annuity and, as usual, advice is necessary.

Unless you have inherited wealth yourself and there is some left, there is no moral obligation whatsoever to pass on your own created residue to your kin. Dee and I inherited nothing substantial apart from small legacies from my mother and Dee's aunt, which we gave away to our children anyway. I therefore feel I am able to spend my own money, including capital, without guilt, for as long as possible.

Dee thinks differently and she would prefer to make life easier for our offspring, if we can afford it. Well, my dear relatives, you may not know what we finally decide until we have died. But, in general, if parents can afford it, I do believe it is better to give money to children while the parent is alive and can therefore enjoy the happy smiles on their children's faces, rather than leave it until the very end with all the relatives squabbling after you are dead and cold.

Summary

Money is a convenient representation of value: value for your work and value for everything you purchase. Money is the lifeblood of day-to-day living, and managing it well means a more contented life. Remember also that happiness is a positive cash flow. It is worth spending some time on mastering the basics of budgeting, house purchase, money management and, eventually, investing.

Analyse every investment from a perspective of risk, reward and flexibility. Genuine risk-free **and** high-return investments do not exist. Make your own mind up after listening to a professional. Never give any adviser total discretion: never hand over control.

Buy a house using a flexible mortgage. Use the reserve, when you can, to build up a buy-to-let portfolio, using income to finance new purchases. Retire on the rent. Invest in an ISA when you can afford it and in a pension linked to tracker funds.

Your first reading of this section might have been somewhat intense. So have a cup of coffee – and try again later on.

Horoscopes, intuition and superstition

Younger readers in particular can easily be influenced by superstition. My objective here is to put these mind games in perspective and to convince you to accept that they are for fun but not for real. This should encourage you to have more confidence in coping with life as it really is, despite erroneous attempts to present it as pre-ordained or constantly affected by a potpourri of occult events.

People like hearing about themselves. It is therefore quite easy to be attracted to horoscopes and many of us are eager to adapt the all-purpose commentary to our own personal life pattern, sometimes stretching credibility to the limit. It is all innocent fun, but also an example of the ability of good horoscope writers to use their experience of human nature to express themselves in a convincing format. It is applied wisdom but used for entertainment purposes.

Horoscopes should not be taken seriously. You know that already really. The zodiac is merely a prop, a useful device for the guru to give the impression that he is only *interpreting* signs from a higher power, much as a priest acts as God's envoy. It is really a convincing piece of fiction, but there are some basic rules followed by the fraternity to ensure consistency when defining characteristics for any given star sign. For example, we Taurus people apparently are always stubborn, solid and earthy. Legions of both good and bad stories could be written about these basic attributes, but the fundamental theme must remain consistent in order to add to the credibility of the ritual.

Unlike horoscopes, clairvoyants interact personally. When you see a good clairvoyant in action, perhaps reading your palm, feeling your head bumps or consulting tarot cards, you see applied wisdom in action. These check. One must be proactive to get wise, not merely reactive. An enthusiasm for living is essential.

Wisdom, and its quest, is fundamental to understanding people and negotiating the complex web of life. While our environment and our technology changes ever more rapidly, the basic nature of human beings remains fairly consistent. Once you have mastered the art of summing up people more accurately, life becomes far easier to plot. As life becomes ever more complex it is essential to interpret the facts wisely.

There will never be a more important time than *now* to make a correct analysis, because I consider the world, and life as we have known it, may well be on a dangerous precipice. I hope there is a solution. I believe there is.

Summary

It is important to differentiate between true wisdom and applied superstition. Experience will demonstrate this, provided you develop an innate sense of constant curiosity, an urge to challenge and to analyse, even what appear to be norms. It helps to make mistakes from time to time, to learn constructive lessons.

Observe, think and conclude. Structure the evidence in a mental database of compartmentalised behaviour models. Hopefully you will then be better able to recognise a familiar pattern out of a future event and thereby reuse the same thinking process. As your database builds and is reconfirmed with actual events, which start to work out more often in practice as predicted, one's self-assurance builds. This experience then becomes applied common sense.

Common sense, plus the confidence to apply it, then gradually turns into true wisdom. It is not always an easy process, nor is it quick; but it is fundamentally necessary if you are to gain the most of what life has to offer.

Medicine and psychiatry

Your state of heath has a somewhat critical significance if you accept that life has to be lived to the full, and for as long as possible. I have some pompous opinions on the subject, which could possibly improve your health, well-being and longevity.

A remarkable fact I have noticed is that the body can perform its own healing more or less automatically without much intervention. Doctors can recommend drugs and procedures to assist the process but the fundamental curative mechanism is in built. Surgeons can of course cut and paste and help us out of some serious problems, but even they ultimately rely on our body's quite astonishing ability to repair itself. The doctor's role seems to consist of keeping the patient contented while nature does the real healing work.

Although good heath and careful living obviously enable a longer, happier life, what do we all do about it in practice? We revel in dangerous activities; we drive at excessive speed, often while mentally impaired; we smoke; we take life-threatening drugs for "fun"; we eat stodgy, unhealthy food. We proclaim boxing a "sport"; and we engage in wars at any opportunity. Why do we have to live so precariously when life has so much more to offer? Yet when the chips are down, we miraculously pull a life-saver out of the bag at the last moment. Someone once said the most dangerous time of life is the first 10 minutes. I believe the last 10 minutes are somewhat more critical!

As I grow older, the need to accept my mortality becomes far more evident. Death is of little concern to the immortal youth who has his whole life in front of him and has this urge to test every boundary. Such adrenaline rushes are pleasurable and sometimes addictive: it is *danger* that gives rise to these euphoric states. Ironically living dangerously can also hone ones basic survival skills, nature's way of building robustness. If a child is cocooned for too long and not exposed to day-to-day bacteria, he will not develop an effective immune system and will thus become more vulnerable to disease. So perhaps nature has it right after all. However, I still believe one has to be selective with one's choice of "dangers".

The longer I live, the more potential danger areas I notice. Having children of your own immediately focuses the mind on life's hazards, and an abrupt change of attitude occurs when becoming a parent. One starts to restrain the kids from excessive adventure (that you once enjoyed yourself) and preaching "safety first" almost to the point of becoming a killjoy. The children take no notice of course. It is a big dilemma for parents who wish to protect their young, yet at the same time wish to see them free and happy and accept that they too need to taste danger so they can recognise it, and develop resilience to cope with life's hazards.

In the introduction I said I would map out some potholes. Here are some to avoid that are sadly not usually considered relevant by the young.

Excessive driving speed clearly kills. So slow down a bit – an extra five minutes to save a life (and not just yours) seems a very good deal to me!

Smoking damages your health – guaranteed. We all intuitively know this, so do not smoke at all – it's a dirty, dangerous habit, which also betrays your lack of self-control. I admit I used to smoke when I was young because I thought it was fashionable and it was part of belonging to a more adult set. Looking back, I realise it was a stupid thing to do.

Eat properly: there is ample evidence now to point us to good eating habits. Unfortunately, the businesses who produce our food and drink know we have a weakness for fatty fast food, alcohol, sugary drinks, chocolate, cakes ... ummm – how true!. Clearly, these companies are unlikely to follow a policy of making their unhealthy products less tasty and attractive – it is bad for business. However, you need not become a sucker for it. Be very selective with what you consume. You are what you eat – if you survive long enough – and only *you* can decide how discerning you want to be. (I wish I had focused on this vital aspect much earlier in my life when I was more lean.)

Exercise is supposed to be good for you – in moderation. My theory is that if you want a piece of machinery to last a long time, you do not put too many miles on the clock. By all means take the thing out for a spin regularly and service it by keeping the moving parts, oiled and, well, moving; but don't wear it out too soon by driving it too hard and too long. Pace the body if you want to cheat nature and stick around a bit longer, particularly if you have mastered the knack of keeping happy for most of the time. Unlike my generation, you will probably live a lot longer and suffer less nasty illnesses, such is the rate of medical progress. But don't count on medical science alone to add years to your life – play safe – run gently and modestly.

Good doctors are hard to find. As I write (in 2004) they are overstretched in a hopelessly overburdened health service where there are more administrators than medical practitioners – ridiculous, isn't it? However, it is usually worth taking advice from a doctor but do not just meekly accept his diagnoses as perfect: be subjective and ask questions. Enquire about the after-effects of drugs; ask about alternative treatments or even take another opinion. It is your body, and your taxes pay for the service.

Do not expect instant cures – that is unfair on the system. There is seldom enough time for a GP to make a full diagnosis, and you sometimes have to be pushy and insistent – in a friendly way of course. Sometimes the body just cannot repair itself. Moreover, medical professionals are not miracle workers, despite some doctors thinking they are gods. Good health is not a right but a hope.

There are some very annoying features about our health service. An enormous amount of money is wasted on unnecessary drugs for people who do not benefit from them. A doctor writes out dozens of prescriptions a day, but how does he, or the medical profession in general, know if they produced the anticipated result? There is no formal mechanism for feedback, except a possible revisit. Often the body cures itself, so it is a mute point whether the recommended drug was helpful or not. Easing pain is clearly desirable, but I believe all patients should be asked to complete a form, or orally assist one being completed by the doctor, before getting their next prescription. This form would summarise the effects, good or bad, of the last prescription.

Just think what such a huge database of symptom and cure could be created, and what enormous benefit it could be for future diagnoses. It is not enough to rely on the drug companies to do the research – the cost is eventually paid by us, the taxpayer anyway. Why not take advantage of the largest free group of guinea pigs – all of us?

Many people forget that antibiotics are *not* effective against viral infections, only against bacteria. We constantly overuse antibiotic drugs "just in case", and then fail to finish the course. This simply increases the chance of developing antibiotic resistance: the little bugs get wise and mutate to a better strain unless they are killed off properly. This is bad news, not just for you, but also for other sufferers from the same problem, who would find themselves using less effective drugs.

Alternatives?

Many alternative health practitioners take advantage of the so-called placebo effect. If you give a patient a harmless sugar pill but tell them it is a new drug that is designed to cure their ailment, surprisingly some 30% of recipients, sometimes more, will report positive effects, even total cures. Pain reduction can often be just as effective after taking a mere placebo, as after taking a conventional analgesic. Researchers for new drugs are well aware of this effect, which is why they operate "double-blind" methods to eliminate the placebo effect. The body mostly self-heals but does it even better if its owner really believes in a specific healing event.

Faith healers rely totally on that very effect. So do other specialists. Some use machines that detect "mineral shortages" by scanning your fingernails with a special apparatus that emits a sound whenever a "discovery" is made. The equipment is actually nothing more than an impedance detector. In skilled hands it can be made to produce any desirable sound with manual pressure depending on what mineral needs to be "suggested". Ironically, it can actually work because of the placebo effect it has on the trusting patient. Sometimes the illness itself is not as serious as the patient imagines and just a little tender loving care can often produce a miraculous cure.

Many alternative practitioners are able to diagnose illness through both intuitive and clinical skills: but a patient's confidence in a cure can be substantially enhanced if it can be associated with some more easily accepted ritual (particularly if combined with some esoteric apparatus) and where the practitioner thinks it works too. The reputation of the serious practitioner will always grow: it has to because inevitably there will be more "cures" reported than failures. This reputation will further enhance the all-important confidence factor.

I think the success of acupuncture has a similar explanation. There are others, such as homeopathy. In general, I think more good than harm is done by alternative practitioners, but I would not dismiss alternative techniques out of hand by any means. Osteopaths and chiropractors, previously thought of as "alternative", are now recognised as professional specialists who can genuinely assist with muscular and back pain.

Conventional doctors must necessarily be more direct and would never be able to declare such confidence to their patients and especially not indulge in any ritualistic treatment. A doctor's natural honesty ironically advances the reputation of the alternative "mystical" set, and the cycle becomes almost self-fulfilling. But please understand how it works and recognise that belief, self-confidence and positive thinking can also come from within without the need for external rites and rituals.

Mental problems?

I will probably upset many people by saying that I think many of the problems described as psychological are in reality self inflicted, and can be cured by a little firmness with oneself. Being depressed is not always a disease in my opinion – it is a state of mind. Psychiatrists who treat this for a living will have their arms waving in the air I am sure – they would do, wouldn't they? Yes, there are of course some serious mental illnesses that need serious treatment. I am just talking about everyday depression here.

Everyone gets down in the dumps from time to time. However, it only gets worse if you allow it to do so. Depression is a continuous feeling of unhappiness caused by unnecessary dwelling on negative things. So, dwell on positive things. Most people from time to time must have experienced a period of depression where there appeared to be no hope. You have too? But clearly you did come out of it – so there *was* hope after all, but you chose to ignore it at the time.

My point is this. If past experience proved that your last depression was temporary, cheer up *now*: why waste time? OK, allow for say a day to sulk and let people know you are a bit despondent to get some sympathy, but then snap out of it and smile. If you feel a depression coming on – take drastic action – think positive things. It really does work.

> "Smile a while, for while you smile, another smiles and soon there's miles and miles of smiles and life's worthwhile: because you smile."

Although Dee learnt that when she was 12, I like the principle – and it is true anyway.

Beware drugs of every sort. Mildly depressed people should particularly avoid *uppers* and *downers* except as a very last resort. All drugs have side-effects. Even so-called homeopathic drugs have some side-effects despite their claim to the contrary. It should be possible, with a little positive thinking, to avoid drugs for so-called mental problems, but you must have decided to be determined to take this attitude *before* you become "ill". It is difficult to preach positive thinking when you are already feeling low.

Drug abuse for social reasons (I am referring to heroin, cocaine etc) is a very, very silly activity indeed. If you have to resort to such artificial stimulants to enjoy life – get another life! Please do not even attempt to experiment. It is a slide into oblivion and can cause irreparable long-term damage. You know in your heart that it is a mug's game, so do not even attempt it. It is a wicked business run by clever but ruthless criminal drugs overlords who have a vested interest in your potential addiction, so do not expect help and guidance from those in the "industry". It is also an industry backed by billions of pounds, yet it causes more harm to the poor and the ignorant than any other activity, including war. If you aspire to live with some degree of style and comfort, it must be a totally drug-free existence.

Mind over matter

I am convinced that melancholy people become ill more often. I am equally convinced that being *positive* and determined in one's mind about curing *any* illness, mental or otherwise, can improve chances of a cure significantly, as demonstrated with the placebo effect and the success of "complementary" medicine as it is now more helpfully called. Even cancer sufferers can up their survival chances simply by imagining little antibodies zapping those nasty cancer cells.

I am not suggesting this concept is a miracle cure – no matter how positive you are, death is inevitable. But I am saying that a positive mind **can** improve one's chances of a cure for illnesses and can prolong life. Recent research is coming to the same conclusion. Ask any experienced old doctor and he will probably nod in agreement.

There is a new fast-growing branch of medicine showing great promise – genetics. Until now, we were unable to change our inherited character and make-up and were stuck with the genes our parents gave us at birth. But now it is possible to determine fundamental defects at gene level and even make changes during our own lives. Stem cell research enables us to mend broken bits previously thought impossible to fix. This type of research is controversial because to some it seems like interfering with God's work. To others, it seems there is a danger of letting loose genetically-modified drugs with unknown long-term effects. The same controversy applies to genetically-modified foods.

I do not yet understand all the elements of this argument, but I do sense that this development is of immeasurable importance to the future quality of our lives and it deserves very serious thought as the benefits could hugely outweigh the risks.

Summary

While many heath problems are self-inflicted, fortunately many are also curable from within too. A positive attitude can, I believe, assist the healing process. Nevertheless professional skills, fallible though they may be, can clearly be vital to life, so take full advantage of whatever is on offer – conventional, alternative or complementary – but query and question any diagnosis and proposed treatment and accept nothing at face value.

Keep an open mind on the extraordinary promise of genetic medicine.

Marriage

I have some ideas on how to choose a long-term live-in partner. In the great scheme of life, procreation is a necessary activity, almost pre-ordained. Historically, marriage has always been the ritual that religiously and lawfully legitimised co-habitation and child production. Some might think it is anachronistic today. Living together seems more flexible to many youngsters, particularly for the more fickle male gender, and why make a lifetime commitment that experience has shown has a 30% chance of failure?

Picking a perfect partner is a lottery. How does one know if a long-term relationship will work out without a proper trial beforehand? Traditional society decreed such trials as morally wrong – but this attitude will increase the possibility of a miserable marriage. If you are lucky enough to pick the right partner, your future will have twice the chance of a happy outcome. I have been very lucky with a long-lasting, happy marriage. I have to admit I cannot associate myself with any special wisdom or clairvoyance, and it was very fortuitous that we found each other. In my case it was love at first sight. I may therefore be biased when I say that marriage is better than co-habitation.

All partners will occasionally squabble, bicker and fight. It is part of the fun, particularly the making-up bit. Relationships that claim "we've never had a cross word in 30 years" may actually not be living life to the full. Unmarried partners will find it easier to part: marriage is a lifetime commitment and this additional moral and legal obligation helps to ensure that occasional rows are temporary rather than permanent.

There are also some tax advantages if you are weighing up the pros and cons. Legal spouses can transfer assets without capital gains tax and, on death, inter-spouse transfers are exempt for capital transfer tax. If a surviving partner always remarries a younger spouse, one could avoid capital transfer tax altogether!

Compatibility to me does not mean you share the same opinions on everything: it means that one person complements the other with strengths where the other is weak. A different viewpoint keeps relationships fresh and lively. No one is perfect (apart from Dee, of course) and everyone makes mistakes throughout their life: it is healthy to admit this to one another when you discover you were wrong (which I was once). I believe that each party should remain true to their views, while allowing for inevitable error, and yet remaining open-minded about their partner's opinions. This approach will ensure an extra-dimensional view on life and an altogether richer relationship. One might say incompatibility is a requirement of compatible partnering. However, there must be a basic mutual respect, so opinions should not be too diverse on personal issues.

Love is a key ingredient to a long-term relationship: when you are in love, you will certainly know what that wonderful and frightening state feels like. Youngsters in love for the first time will experience an overwhelming euphoria: the object of your attentions will be total perfection in absolutely everything and you will immediately want to run away together, abandoning parents and friends and future prospects – just to be together. Yes. It sounds very romantic. It happens. Sometimes it works out as it did with Dee and me, so how can I argue against it? Moreover, love can grow over the years and provide that indefinable inner glow of mutual contentment, security and trust. Mature love is unbeatable. Strong relationships are unconditional. People can detect it and hanker after it. I wish I could distill the formula to pass on to you. All I can say is that if you are lucky enough to find it, don't lose it.

A South African psychologist acquaintance of ours suggested that potential partners should consider their potential long-term "companionship rating" under eight headings. Fail in three or more and there may be trouble ahead:

1. Religion – a Jew marrying a Muslim *could* be difficult.
2. Sex – preferably opposite – and clearly compatible. Trial helpful!
3. In-laws – should all get on reasonably well on both sides.
4. Money – who earns what and agreed policy for the future.
5. Sociability – recluses and party-lovers may not mix – a sense of humour is usually important.

6. Habits – any nasty ones – amnesty time for reporting any is now!
7. Children – you should share similar views.
8. Work – compatible schedules.

Each area should be discussed in some depth. Communication skills are very important. Relationships without proper communication are likely to founder. The above eight headings are all pretty straightforward and really need no further discussion from me. I have to add that marriage is such an important step since it is a *lifetime* you are planning and not just a *wedding*. Take time and care in your choice of partner. Shotgun marriages are out, unless most of the eight headings above have a satisfactory answer for each of you.

Interestingly, *friendship* can be looked at as a sort of platonic marriage although few of those eight headings would be an appropriate measure. True friends are rare and usually small in number, whereas one might have hundreds of acquaintances. True friendship is unconditional, which means that you accept differences of attitude and lifestyle, no matter how annoying: despite those differences, such friends possess a bond of mutual likeability and respect; you have shared many experiences together and simply enjoy each other's company from time to time.

Friends are almost as important as live-in partners. It is always a pleasurable experience to wine and dine with good, easy, close friends and chuckle over the events of the world, and chat about, well, everything. Living without friends is like having chips without vinegar – so add a bit of spice to life and deliberately search out some really good friends.

Marriages occasionally get seriously fraught and divorce is threatened. Usually problems arise over misunderstandings and lack of honest communication. Sometimes a relationship can drift into a routine where romance becomes stale and mutual esteem for those original aspirations, so fresh, passionate and exciting at the start, falls away. If this seems to be happening to you, talk, listen and be determined to rekindle what you know was once a fire. Check out the above eight headings once more and work at it. Good relationships are worth fighting for; never expect life to be easy all the time. Even an infidelity, the ultimate betrayal, can be conceded, provided the reasons are discussed, forgiveness is asked for and given.

If divorce is inevitable, do it with good mutual grace. You clearly loved each other once. Hating now, being obstructive and difficult with regard to access to children and so on out of spite does no good to anyone. Try to stay friends whatever. It will be happier for everyone, including in-laws and obviously for any children. Remember also that if you cheat on your partner, supposedly your best friend, you could cheat on anyone: not a desirable attribute or reputation. Talk before you walk.

Finally, have children if you are able. Not necessarily immediately. Careers are important and there are many stresses and strains on a new couple: children are one of them. Children need both parents and their arrival heralds a surprising, new outlook on life for both of you. Eventually you will have grandchildren – even better, as you can then leave the messy bits to their parents. If I knew then what I know now, I think I would only have had grandchildren …

Sex

Sex is yet another wonderful gift of nature, primarily as an incentive to reproduce, but great fun all the same. I will not say much about this deeply personal subject except this. It **is** deeply personal, and very intimate. I suggest you keep it that way.

There is a modern tendency to flaunt overt sexual behaviour in the media, in "reality" TV programmes and the like. Too much exposure desensitises and can destroy a brilliant piece of nature's magic. Slow discovery is more wondrous than wham, bang, thank you ma'am. Females love being *loved* more than anything else: they will please their partner well beyond expectations, if loved. Girls – please note that men do not always go for over-obvious glamour and excessive cleavage. Sex appeal is more about what you keep in reserve rather than what you flaunt. Males worry about their performance – but, guys, gentle, thoughtful loving is superior to mere athletic performance. Experiment by all means, variation is often appealing and good at sustaining interest but remember it is ultimately an act of love. To give pleasure is ultimately more deeply satisfying than to take it.

Similarly, discussion with anyone other than your partner also tends to affect the magic of sex. Even too much analysis with your partner could turn a loving act into a clinical one. Keep it intimate and loving and not cheap and smutty.

Men are from Mars and women from Venus

This is the title of a popular book about gender differences and is definitely worth a read. Despite its mass appeal, it is also remarkably accurate. Essentially, men and women are not just physically different but think very differently too, despite what the politically correct brigade think of sexual equality –genders are *very* different indeed.

For example, men are mainly problem-solvers. Women usually like to be cosseted and talked to. A woman with a problem is not just looking for a solution but someone to share the problem. This is not a sexist joke – it is actually true. Women have more empathy, and are more caring with others and bring up children more effectively. Women talk to other women about their problems. Men keep problems to themselves and aggressiveness is higher up the option list of solutions.

There are numerous other examples and I say *vive la difference*, for this is the very spice of life. What a bore if we were the same. You just cannot treat, deal with, negotiate with or live with the opposite gender in any way the same as you would the same gender. Read the book – it is naff in parts but worthy despite that. It should certainly increase your chance of a happier and more successful relationship with the opposite sex.

Being gay

I have nothing against gays or lesbians. They can be more sensitive human beings than heterosexuals. However, it is a sad status, since the prime purpose of life – passing on the proverbial baton – is evidently precluded.

If you or your friends are gay, I have this message. I commend you to respect the world for what it is – mostly heterosexual: it has evolved that way and cannot evolve further without it being so.

Please do not try to compel others to be more compatible with your lifestyle, which is different from that which nature intended. I do not object to how you choose to live as long as it is private. I do not like to see marches for gay rights, gay marriages and proclamations for equality. Use your legendary empathy to recognise that your orientation is not equal, but will be more than amply tolerated if it is kept private and personal.

Summary

Marriage can be a great institution with the right partner: partner selection needs care and some luck. Try the eight-point test listed above. Children will change your life but are what life is about. Read the next section about bringing up children.

Take some time and trouble to understand the opposite gender. They are more different than you first thought; making appropriate allowances for this will certainly improve the quality of your relationships.

Giving pleasure can deliver a better personal feeling than taking it.

Bringing up children

When we become a parent, we all start out as amateurs. School seldom covers this subject properly – at least not in my day. Raising children properly is not easy yet is one of the more crucial activities in our lives. There are many books on the subject, but let me opine about some principles that I believe in. I will start with the following well-known anonymous homily.

Children learn what they live

If a child lives with criticism, he learns to condemn.
If a child lives with hostility, he learns to fight.
If a child lives with ridicule, he learns to be shy.
If a child lives with shame, he learns to feel guilty.
If a child lives with tolerance, he learns to be patient.
If a child lives with encouragement, he learns confidence.
If a child lives with praise, he learns to appreciate.
If a child lives with fairness, he learns justice.
If a child lives with security, he learns to have faith.
If a child lives with approval, he learns to like himself.
If a child lives with acceptance and friendship, he learns to find love in the world!

This rather monotonous poem simply suggests that children sometimes emulate their parents. Certainly, good, thoughtful, caring parents can bring up like-minded children. Again, like so many homilies, they are so easy to say and write, and they sound warm and wise, but are not always so straightforward in practice. Try my more cynical version:

> *If a child lives with some criticism*, he learns how to analyse and improve.
> *If a child lives with some hostility*, he learns how to fight back occasionally
> *If a child lives with occasional ridicule*, he learns determination to be better
> *If a child lives with deserved shame*, he learns personal honesty.
> *If a child lives with excessive tolerance*, he learns that standards are not meaningful
> *If a child lives with too much encouragement*, he wonders if he can manage alone
> *If a child lives with constant praise*, he becomes conceited.
> *If a child lives with consistent fairness*, he could misunderstand the real world.
> *If a child lives with too much security*, he becomes weak and scared.
> *If a child lives with general approval*, he learns to like himself and trust himself.
> *If a child lives with acceptance and friendship*, he learns to find there are many good things in the world!

The message here is that life is not always a bed of roses, and children must learn that. However, in my view, much of the original version remains a worthwhile set of general principles – as long as a touch of realism, as set out in version two, is also adopted.

For example, *constant* criticism is indeed unhealthy, but equally *no* criticism at all subdues personal introspection and self-analysis, which is important for a learning child anxious to test out newly-discovered behaviour traits: some are good; some are bad. Without any constructive criticism, how will they know the difference?

I believe that explanations for adult behaviour should be given to children at all stages, simplified, but honest nevertheless. If an adult is angry with a child and then leaves that anger unexplained, to fester and hang like an unwelcome black cloud, the child will be confused. Everyone makes mistakes and everyone occasionally displays unpleasant emotions that they often regret later. A good parent would explain this imperfection.

Children should be allowed to go through their childhood at a natural pace and not be encouraged to be adult too soon. I have noticed a trend to dress kids up in adult ways, so that 10-year-old girls can be made to look like young tarts. Discovering adulthood and losing innocence should be gradual and not sudden. A young mind could easily be polarised and hardened in an undesirable direction simply because it has been exposed to themes or concepts it is ill equipped to judge. Parents have a natural tendency to show off their children: but please do not present them as either too advanced or even too babyish for their actual years.

Children remember parts of their childhood when older, sometimes with stunning clarity, sometimes sub-consciously. In the absence of a clear idea as to how to deal with a particular situation, the sub-conscious will often recall what father did and act accordingly. I remember berating my kids for taking bottled drinks in the house without asking. I should have adopted a friendlier attitude, but my step-father used to say to me that all drinks in the house were his and not mine, and only when I could afford to buy my own could I help myself. It was probably a good lesson, but not how I would have wanted to give it. However, my sub-conscious memory of how my parents dealt with it took over and I replicated the over-heavy admonishment without thinking.

It is worth noting children will always remember their parent's behaviour and use it later as an unconscious aide-memoir in cases of doubt. So behave yourself as you would like your offspring to behave.

Children often turn into adults with interests and talents quite different from those of their parents. Although a child shares its parents' genes, do not be surprised if it has attributes that may not necessarily have shown up in the parents. Dormant genes can occasionally skip a generation. Allow a child time to discover its own abilities and preferences without forcing it to follow the parents' expectations and lifestyle.

One of the most important human attributes is honesty, tempered with a bit of tact in the appropriate circumstances. Being accurate with reality, as opposed to being economical with the truth, is a very much easier code of living. One lie invariably leads to another to cover the first and soon you are caught in a web where the original need for it all is forgotten. Exaggeration is a form of dishonesty, which soon comes home to roost, as people will inevitably find you out. Teach children to be straight and honest by being straight and honest.

A danger of over-discipline is that it encourages untruthfulness to avoid punishment. It is difficult to suggest a rule of thumb, and I have not always got it right, but I think that showing kindness and love to one's children, together with a good explanation of where any transgression lay and why it was wrong, is often better than a physical slap. If children know that they has upset their loving parents, that alone is often sufficient admonition.

Choosing a school has been mentioned elsewhere under "Education". The point made in that section was that children not only emulate their parents, but also their school colleagues. Choose with great care. Private education is not an option if you cannot afford it – and it costs **a lot** – so living in the right area (ie with good schools) is a necessity.

For example, at Wellington College the headmaster pursued the principle that every boy or girl is talented in *something*: the school's aim was to find it, and foster it. That is a good attitude but not one that can be so easily followed in state schools if there are a lack of facilities to deal with a wider range of talents.

Summary

Children should be encouraged to find out what they enjoy and what they are good at. It is not urgent. Given time, this discovery will one day simply emerge. Every child is different and may have a very different skill-set from those of his/her siblings. Discovering what it is will eventually form the seed that sets off their big life plan. Children must end up doing what they like and are good at – not what their parents insist upon. Round pegs must go into round holes: forcing them into square holes might damage both the peg and the hole.

Parents must not be overprotective and must not be taken in by so-called PC (politically correct) no-no's, such as no admonishing your child. As long as parenting is proactive and not passive, clear explanations are given and that parents practice what they preach, their offspring will one day grow up to be fine human beings.

Good manners

"Manners maketh man".

Remember that saying? It is the motto of both Winchester College and New College, Oxford. As a kid, I used to think it was a load of nonsense and rather prissy. But now I'm 14, going on 60 something, I would like to take a moment (you too please) to explain why I think manners and etiquette are actually very important.

First, an important fact: the emotional side of our psyche is a far more powerful motivator than the intellect. People actually *do* judge a book by its cover, or favour a car by its colour and prefer clothes in vogue with the latest fashion fad. Whether a book was a good read, a car is well built or clothes actually fit is quite often secondary, despite a consumer reticence to admit this logic-lapse. People often choose a product because of its emotional appeal rather than its functionality. A *feeling* will often sway an opinion more than a *fact*. Rightly or wrongly, it pays to understand that the motivators behind human interaction are not just logical but emotional as well, and sometimes even rather superficial.

Good manners essentially display thoughtfulness for others. By demonstrating your skill and knowledge of etiquette and inter-personal protocol, you show others that you are a considerate and empathetic person, rather than a selfish lout. Often good manners are simply a matter of good taste. While some rituals may seem over elaborate, it is more the lack of any that marks you out as a less thoughtful, less caring person, or as one in the wrong social group. If you wish to be seen as an oaf, just ignore good manners.

If you prefer to present a more sophisticated image, there are ways of acting which send the appropriate message. Some protocols betray your upbringing. For example, if you hold your knife like a pencil, the chances are you have come from a typical working class background. Grasping a knife in a cutting position is taught in more middle class families. There is nothing right or wrong with either method; neither am I suggesting that working class families do not bring up children "correctly". It happens to be a particular mannerism that seems to be class related.

Similarly, good speech is the mark of a caring upbringing. Children usually emulate their parents' vernacular. Care in pronunciation immeasurably improves the ability to impart a clear message. Slang, sloppy sentences and missing consonants will debase our otherwise very rich and comprehensive English language. Accents are also important and good ones can be acquired. A natural accent is often a pleasure and seldom causes offence. However, an evidently artificial accent, which attempts to emulate old royalty, or what has been termed the *Sloane accent*, is just so obviously false that it creates the impression of inanity, and should be avoided.

Use of some words can reveal one's upbringing as well. For example, *napkin* is middle class, as opposed to *serviette* which isn't; or *the loo* as opposed to *the toilet*; *dinner* when you mean *lunch*; *How d'you do?* as opposed to *Pleased to meet you*. There are hundreds more. Usage of different words and expressions to describe the same thing is not in itself right or wrong: it simply indicates your upbringing. I am the first to lambaste people who try to pretend they are something they are not. But it is a perfectly legitimate practice to improve one's elocution and to adopt the normal mannerisms and protocols of the social group you choose to be in. Just because you were born in a family, which, say, dropped their *gees* (goin' instead of going), and *aitches* ('aircut instead of haircut) doesn't mean you shouldn't try to improve your pronunciation. That is not pretending to be what you are not. Presentation is everything. Creating the right impression is an important attribute in any inter-personal relationship, at work or at play, so it makes good sense to adopt an appropriate image to match with the sort of person you wish people to perceive. If you wish to join a particular club, you are expected to follow the rules, unwritten or not. I am not saying that everyone must speak perfect Queen's English, but there is no disgrace in trying to improve this vital communication skill.

The female gender is usually more attracted to a well-mannered male because he displays care and thoughtfulness towards her. Some useful traits are worth developing even though some might appear to be dying out. Opening a door for a lady is one obvious example. Standing up when a lady stands or leaves a room or a table is a classic mannerism, albeit seldom seen these days, but is never actually out of place for the lady in question. I still feel uncomfortable sitting in a seat on public transport when a woman (of any age) is forced to remain standing. There are many obvious physical reasons for these rituals that remain timeless and I believe should be encouraged. There are some males who say it's old-fashioned and even some women who feel it is sexist. I disagree. And most *feminine* ladies would too.

From the ladies' point of view, I would urge them to show approval and encouragement of any vestige of good manners that might be displayed by a male. We would all like to appear to be more civilised than the mere animals from which we originated. Supporting good manners and politeness is an excellent start.

Fashion

I have never been very fashionable personally, particularly in the sartorial sense – but Dee sorts me out there. Females are far more conscious of dress and style. However, there are certain extremes that I find difficult to tolerate. Men wearing jewellery such as earrings or medallions are just too much for me. Tattoos are bad enough on men, but on women – yuck!

Multi-coloured hairstyles, trendy only on planet Mars, and body piercing in the most bizarre places, are only *cool* to teenagers anxious to project an image of rebelliousness – any style will do as long as it is not what parents or teachers wear or expect to see. Being in vogue may be part of a natural desire to be seen as a member of "hip" society, but there are limits and there is good fashion and awful "fashion". Please grow out of the awful stage quickly, and do not do anything permanent to your body, as you will certainly regret it later.

Dress sense is also a question of good manners in that it shows thought for others to dress appropriately. Turning up at a funeral flaunting a tee-shirt displaying in large letters "Fcuk Fashion" does not exactly exhibit much respect for the deceased and their grieving family. If in doubt as to what to wear, think of what your host would prefer. Dee reckons that good taste is a question of observation and analysis of those people who have that certain, attractive style, then adapting what you observed to your own body shape, size and hair colour. She says that it is better to have a small wardrobe of good quality clothes than a large collection of cheapies. Sounds right to me. A decent suit and tie for a man can seldom be wrong for any occasion, apart from perhaps a beach party where the tie might be a little over-the-top!

Being sociable

While on the subject of parties, I am all for a good time – and as often as possible – and I do not always wear a suit and tie these days. I like my birthdays to spread over a week. Having a pleasant meal with good friends is better than dining alone. I did not always think this way. When I was younger and very dedicated to my business, I had no time for socialising, unless I was able to pontificate to captive guests about my latest ideas. I was the classic bore. It was not only selfish and bad mannered, but it won me few real friends during that intense period. I put it down euphemistically to "being shy" or, better still, "over enthusiastic". Nonsense of course: I am ashamed to say it was just boorish conceit!

Dee was always the perfect hostess, listened to everyone with patient care, asked interesting questions and was generally a marvellous conversationalist. Her main secret was simply showing interest in the other person. It seems so obvious today, and I try now to listen more than speak. I still fail on occasion ("most occasions!" says my loving spouse) but I hope to be better when I am more grown up. It's also not always easy to listen when you are deaf. What?

Summary

People often judge a book by its cover or a film by its trailer. It is important that **your** cover is well presented. Being perceived as a polite, well-spoken, well-mannered, well-dressed and caring person, following the required protocols of the society in which you wish to cohabit is a key skill well worth acquiring. It improves your chances of success in everything you do, including attracting the opposite sex. It also makes you feel better about yourself.

It is not being prissy after all.

Gambling and other addictions

Having an addiction of any sort inevitably results in a very sad and unhappy state for both the addict and their families. Unfortunately, many young people can slip into addiction if they have not been made aware of its dangers.

It is always a depressing sight to observe the sort of people going in and out of bookies (turf accountants). They have the aura of the loser about them. And of course they *are* losers. There are many people who crave financial success but, rather than work for it, a lucky win seems to be so much easier and eventually their life depends on it. They borrow from friends thinking their luck must change: borrowing turns to stealing as they lose their friends. In the end, they lose not just money but self-respect and even the support of their family.

There are no long-term winning punters in the horseracing game or in the gambling casinos. There are no "systems" that guarantee success. It is simple mathematics.

Take something simple like roulette. The wheel has 37 slots – numbered 1 to 36 plus a zero – sometimes even a double zero. Therefore, the chances of picking the winning slot are 1 in 37. However, if you win, you get paid only 36 times your stake. This means that, on average, you lose a 37th of your stake, or about 2.7%, on each and every spin. Add that up over a period and you can soon see why it is worth *owning* a casino!

Roulette also offers elusively attractive betting alternatives: reds or blacks, odd or even numbers, doubles and so on, but the odds **all** favour the casino. It's OK to have a bit of fun and you might be lucky but, over a period, you cannot be ahead unless you are exceedingly lucky: very few are. I have never met one.

Gamblers look on their addiction differently. I have seen some avid punters writing down the result of each wheel spin, attempting to discern a pattern: "five reds in succession – that must favour a black on the next spin". Total nonsense of course. In reality, the chances of winning are identical every spin – just 18 out of 37 for even bets – quite regardless of previous spins. If it was 18 out of 36, you might just break even: that little extra slot makes all the difference and guarantees that the casino wins in the long term – obviously.

Horse racing is even more loaded against the punter, and yet still people believe they might know the odds better than the professional bookmaker. The sad fact about gambling in general is that it not only affects a larger number of people than you might think, but almost all of them are from the poorer, less-educated communities. The few high rollers who ought to know better can afford to drop a few grand, but when you start out with almost nothing you very quickly become desperate. The government support it because of the taxes they earn, regardless of the misery it causes. Gambling attracts criminals because they are streetwise and they understand, better than most, the weaknesses of the poor and the ignorant.

Drinking and drug-taking are other addictions that affect the poor more than the rich, since they produce a temporary euphoria to make up for life's beastliness. Contented people have no need of drugs or excessive booze unless they are greedy for such dead-end experiences. There are more illnesses and accidents related to alcohol than any other disease, yet the government happily collects billions in duty from the drinks industry.

Please do not misunderstand me: I am not suggesting Prohibition as happened in the 1920s in America, and which simply pushed the problem underground into the hands of criminals. Quite the reverse. I believe we should legalise most drugs in order to eliminate the unregulated criminal pushers who have a vested interest in addiction. A regulated distribution will take away the teenager's exhilaration in doing something illegal, and eventually the distribution would end up more like sad betting shops that most self-respecting citizens would eventually ignore. It would then be up to the public to decide for themselves, subject to a massive advertising campaign highlighting the idiocy of gambling, drinking to excess and taking drugs.

It is a far more complex dilemma than I have suggested here and I have no pat answers: but I have observed what addiction can do to people and their families and it is far from pleasant. Governments have a duty to act with some urgency.

As far as my reader is concerned, I hope you have grasped my point – addiction is not nice and is a slippery slope to oblivion. Don't even step on the slide. Don't even experiment. There are far better things in life yearning for your attention.

Summary

An addiction for gambling, drink or drugs is one of life's major, nasty potholes, which must be avoided at all costs. I believe these addictions stem from some personality weakness. Parents have a duty to watch for it and stamp on it early. Never feed it by paying off the inevitable debts. The constant heart-wrenching dilemma of whether to settle children's gambling debts or drug bills can be a never-ending struggle. Families often suffer more than the addict does. Although it hurts, one must initially be cruel to be kind.

An addict of any description always has a personal agenda that is seldom disclosed to anyone else. There is always a reason, a pay-off of some description to explain any bizarre action. Identifying it to the addict and gaining his/her acceptance of change may offer some hope.

Professional help is available for both victim and families, but it requires the addict to have the strength of character to do something about it. If you feel you suffer yourself, get a really strong grip of yourself as otherwise you may ruin your whole life. There appears to be no medical solution – it must ultimately come from within the victim's own mind and personal determination.

Staying alive for as long as possible – personal security

Have you ever noticed these strange phenomena: whenever animals or insects seem to be under threat, they never seem to notice until the very last second. Dogs run in front of cars, flies buzz around cobwebs, antelopes nonchalantly feed just yards from hungry lions, all seemingly oblivious of the greatly increased chance of their imminent, unpleasant death. I can only assume they rely on some very basic, simple instinct rather than trying to think through the increasing danger and moving away from it earlier.

But we humans are supposed to have brains. We should be able detect danger and arrive at a plan of action to minimise the threat. Of course, life has always been a lottery and anyone, regardless of his or her care, can be vulnerable to unpredictable and sudden catastrophe. It is difficult to dodge a drunken driver suddenly veering across the road and smashing into you head on. However, if we value our life, we can better the odds with a bit of extra thought and planning.

Even intelligent humans still do stupid things like building a house on an earthquake fault line (eg California), or building a town near the sea but under sea level and in a hurricane zone (eg New Orleans). Youngsters seldom want to see danger because, to them, life is a voyage of exciting discovery. Old crinklies like me who have "been there and done that" (and forgotten some of it) have a better sense of judgement for potential perils. Even simple things, such as allowing extra time to travel to an important meeting to account for traffic jams, are born out of actual experience. Can I pass down some very basic ideas for minimising dangers?

Many imminent perils give clear signs in advance, so that proper action (or possibly no action) can occur. A bad weather forecast should deter amateur sailors from setting off in the first place. One must learn how to listen out for all the danger signals, to take note of them, and think through the consequences. Another example: there is usually ample time to pick up warning signs of impending major strikes (or even wars) and then decide what to do about them. Basic requirements – fuel, food and water – can run short even in the most advanced countries for sometimes bizarre reasons, or simply because of a national strike. So heed the signs when they arise and do not ignore them.

Stocking up with long-term foodstuffs is not a bad idea in such an emergency, as long as you turnover your store from time to time to prevent it going out of date. I also keep a generator in case of prolonged electricity outages. It is surprising how much of the home relies on electricity. Even a gas boiler is controlled electrically. A small generator may not be able to replace the full mains current, but it can certainly operate vital, selective items one at a time and can charge batteries.

A few jerry cans of stored petrol can facilitate an urgent journey. Dee always fills up with petrol at a journey's end rather than at the beginning of the next journey – the next journey may be an emergency trip in the middle of the night during a petrol strike! Torches and battery radios are pretty essential items – in an emergency, news will come by radio. Don't rely on the phone network, particularly mobiles which are the first to jam up in an emergency. Mobile phones are clearly useful but for the really security conscious, a satellite phone does not rely on the cellular network.

Gas cookers (and gas), medical supplies and a first-aid kit is an obvious item to have at all times. A cash stash is useful should the banks be on strike. Filling each bath with water (for drinking or cooking) is a good step too.

On a less dramatic scale, ensure you have your contacts list readily available – friends and contacts are pretty important during an emergency. It is helpful to have several copies, eg on a PDA, a mobile phone and a laptop. Your children should be similarly equipped.

Violence is all around us. There is little doubt that, in the short term, strong violence will win in practically all cases – a handful of might inevitably overcomes a bag full of right. Unless you are built like Sylvester Stallone and with SAS training, there is little chance of winning a fight against determined opposition, armed with knives or other weapons. You cannot talk yourself out of a threat from someone hyped up with drugs. I am not suggesting cowardice – just plain common sense: run away or give in. It is not worth risking your life just for a stolen wallet, a mobile phone or even a few hundred pounds. Better still, avoid potentially dangerous areas in the first place.

People can become very self-centred during a real emergency and anarchy is never far away. You must be able to make a plan for you and your family and accept that the normal laws may have to be stretched in certain circumstances. One must remain vigilant, make a plan for safety as a priority, and then plan to move to a more secure environment with food, water and shelter. Share your plan with your loved ones.

It is possible to suggest strategies for almost every conceivable emergency and there are numerous books on the subject. I am no expert in emergency procedures, but my aim here is to warn you of the importance of being alert to what is happening at all times, to predict possible outcomes and to make a plan accordingly. Ensure the basic ingredients for survival are to hand and that contingency plans are made in advance. These ingredients include communications equipment as well as basic life-sustaining items (ie food and water, warmth, shelter and medicines). These vulnerable supplies could collapse quickly and you cannot always rely upon the state to come to your rescue.

The government have a simple emergency policy: Go in, Stay in, Tune in. There is an agreement with radio and TV companies that if there is a major emergency they will interrupt programming to give public safety advice and information about the incident, so that when you tune in locally or nationally anywhere in the UK you'll get the advice you need. A battery or wind-up radio, is therefore essential. I would however temper the government policy with an element of independence – if it becomes clear that you need to move out – then **move**.

Summary

When you have an idle moment, occasionally, just think what might go wrong in your world, make some contingency plans, and share them with your family.

Death

Death happens. It is unavoidable despite my desire to live forever. How should you handle it?

My penalty for being a non-believer in heaven is absolute, eternal death: the end, finale, finish, over and out, ashes to ashes and that's it. No heaven, no hell, just unperceived peace and silence – for ever.

It is not to be feared but I do try not to dwell on it too much. My opinions are simple: respect the dead, partake in funeral rituals and pray as others do, regardless of your personal beliefs: this is not the time to display indifference to God. To many mourners present, religion is all the comfort they might get for the passing over of loved ones. This is not the time to mock religious protocols.

Some bereaved sufferers believe they can still make contact with their deceased relatives. I personally do not believe this to be possible. However, if it gives comfort to some people, there is little point in abusing their beliefs. They will come to their own decision about it in their own time.

While I may not fear my own inevitable death, as such, I do fear for the death of my wife and family. The pain would be unimaginable. I cannot perceive life without Dee and she thinks the same about me. One resolution is simply to go together, but that seems like being selfish to our children and grandchildren, unless it is an accident.

I much regret to say that although I have opinions and solutions to most of the today's problems, I have no answer at all as to how to relieve the pain of a loved one's death. If ever there would become a time to reconsider my religious views, it might well be in this dire situation: as I write, I honestly feel that all the positive thinking in the world would fail me in this particular extreme state and I would want to end my own life too. It is probably silly and illogical but it is a powerful and unexplainable emotion: I guess I must leave it at that.

I should like to be remembered after my death, but when I am dead, I am no longer in a position to think or feel *anything* personally, so it is a wasted thought. However, thinking about it beforehand does provide some comfort and purpose.

My instinctive rationale in living is to keep alight the gift of life presented to me by my parents for as long as it takes to pass that all important baton of life on to my offspring. They will pick it up and continue onwards the same way, taking the genes that I myself inherited and combined with Dee's to produce them. They will then blend their own genes with their own choice of partner, and so our life continues in them. If they choose well, our descendents will be better than before in every respect. That is the purpose of life. That is my legacy. My body may die but my soul and Dee's soul remain inextricably alive within our descendents as DNA. That is sufficient remembrance for me.

Final summary

You have probably had your fill of **my** opinions by now, and are possibly anxious to pen your own. I have some years still to go and may well live to regret some of these words. However, a brief summary of what I have been saying is as follows:

1. Who are we? We are transient animals with better thinking and communication mechanisms than all the rest of the living entities in our world. We are probably the master animal but we exist purely to reproduce the next generation. The purpose of life may be just life itself but the journey can be joyous and fulfilling. Make every day count.
2. Religion is a convenient and comfortable concept for many people. I do not follow it, and believe only that death is final. However, religion has become a major lifestyle for a huge number of people, and it cannot be ignored as a significant force for both good and evil. Dee believes that living a good life, prioritising caring for others, thoughtfulness and honesty is a religion itself: I like that idea – it sounds better than being a bland agnostic. Deeism is the answer.
3. A large proportion of terrorists today are Islamic. Fundamentalists are very dangerous and very angry with us for being "ignorant, interfering, decadent infidels". The West has exploited the Arabs for their oil and has so far failed to fully understand the Muslim people. Islam is not just a religion, it is a way of life and much of it based on good principles. Religious beliefs are founded on faith and not logic. Respect for the faith of others is crucial to good world relations. The West has botched it up thus far. I urge you to do all

you can to rectify this ignorance. We must all live in the hope of a war-less solution and the core of the answer lies in understanding and respecting others.

4. Politics is an attitude to life, often affected by upbringing. I personally empathise with the idealistic left but recognise that everyone has different skills and aspirations. So in reality, I think it is right wing theory and action that achieve the optimum for everyone, tempered with care and respect for the individual. At the time of writing, New Labour looks dangerous, pedalling more dishonest "spin" than real good deeds: it is important to consider each party's doctrine very carefully before voting. However, please vote for someone – do not ignore politics.
5. Understanding people requires years of observation, as what you see initially is not always what you finally get. Psychologists separate people into either extroverts (talkers) or introverts (thinkers): In reality, most of us have an element of both, and we can change our basic personality but not our inherited nature.
6. Happiness is a relative state not an absolute one. Almost anyone can be happy regardless of everything. It is a knack, an acquired skill, derived primarily from a positive outlook on life. Play up the good bits and play down the bad. Seize it now. Contentment is a longer-term goal and can be enjoyed by achieving your aims and being satisfied.
7. Fail to plan and you plan to fail. Organise your life so your dreams become basic objectives in a daily time-priority list. Weed out unrealistic ambitions. Face up to problems: never run from them; rather, turn them into advantages. Solve problems objectively and dispassionately by considering the advantages and disadvantages of various courses open to you. The emotional aspect is a very relevant factor in the courses open but not in the actual analysis.
8. Happiness is a positive cash flow. Budgeting can be fun: unpayable debt is always miserable. Mr Micawber says so too.
9. Education eases life's journey, enriches it and enhances pleasure. If you have missed out when you were young for any reason, you can still make up for lost time regardless of age. However, make sure your ambitions match your skill set.
10. If you have the skills listed in the entrepreneur section, promote yourself to the boss and become a tycoon. There is no better feeling than controlling your own destiny and turning your plans into reality.

11. If you do start a business, learn some principles such as those listed in the section on running a business. Read some good management books. Listen to those who have been there before.
12. Understand that horoscopes are for fun and are not alternatives for wise thinking. Gain wisdom through constant curiosity, questioning and analysis. Ignore superstitions – they are all bunkum!
13. Doctors and their medicines do not always cure you if you become ill: the body mostly heals itself. A positive mental attitude can enhance the prospects of healing. Alternative and complementary health can be helpful as it catalyses the positive thinking necessary for successful treatment, despite the rituals offered often being just that – rituals. Good health is paramount. Look after your body: it's a wonderful contraption but it is mortal. Do not abuse it or over use it. Genetics medicine has prospects.
14. Marriage is a serious and wonderfully worthwhile state. Test your mutual suitability by discussing in depth the eight headings listed in the Marriage section in more detail: religion, sex, in-laws, money, sociability, habits, children and work. Communicate often. Have a family. Love them all lots and lots.
15. Bringing up children is not easy – we are all amateur parents initially. But the key is discovering what each child excels in and loves doing and then fostering it, rather than forcing them into something the parent might think is "suitable". Children ultimately remember their parental upbringing and instinctively set their base standards from those of their parents; so live as you would wish them to, since they learn from your lifestyle. Whenever you admonish your child, always explain why.
16. The basic principles of investment, finance and mortgages are similar to most life situations. Everyone wants high performance, flexibility and total safety. The reality is always compromise. Where there is gain there may be pain. Buy in gloom and sell in boom remains the simplest and most effective rule of thumb. Beware high-return low-risk propositions – they may be too good to be true.

    As I write, flexible mortgages (for many people) are far and away the best loan deal of all, as they also provide the perfect answer for a good short-term investment with total flexibility and tax efficiency as well as providing a reserve fund for any purpose.

    You need not give self-created wealth away. Spend it first. But if you must give it away, do it when you are still alive and can directly observe and enjoy the happiness it might hopefully bring.

17. People often judge others from first impressions. Make it a good impression. Good manners display your thoughtfulness for others. Ritual manners and social norms are essential if you intend to thrive in a particular environment relevant to your own aims and ambitions.
18. Be prepared for emergencies and attend to personal security.
19. Death seals the passing of life's baton from one generation to the next. The "soul" lives on in the form of genes inherited from your ancestors. "The King is dead. Long live the King" is an expression I have only recently recognised as being very succinct to the continuation of life.

This little book was designed to identify some of the potholes in life's great journey and to serve as a pocket atlas for the trip. There are probably many other facets I have not dealt with, but I hope I have identified some of the important ones. If I have to add a last sentence it is this:

I can but point – it is up to you to look – and act accordingly.

Over and Out from him...but (inevitably) a final quote from her:

Dee's Dream Recipe for a Piece of Cake

First take one big dream.
Add in some Reality.
Sieve carefully and reduce down until the mixture becomes clear.
Mix in plenty of Drive, Ambition & Confidence: use heaps of Energy and Determination.
Spice with Integrity and Character.
Cook enthusiastically, tasting often until the consistency is just right.
Cut into generous proportions and serve with Care.

With the right mixture, life is just a Piece of Cake!